THE PRESENT AND THE PAST

THE PRESENT AND THE PAST

by

I. COMPTON-BURNETT

LONDON
VICTOR GOLLANCZ LTD
1972

ISBN 0 575 01416 4

Printed in Great Britain by
The Camelot Press Ltd, London and Southampton

CHAPTER I

"Oh, dear, oh, dear!" said Henry Clare.

His sister glanced in his direction.

"They are pecking the sick one. They are angry because it is ill."

"Perhaps it is because they are anxious," said Megan, looking at the hens in the hope of discerning this feeling.

"It will soon be dead," said Henry, sitting on a log with his hands on his knees. "It must be having death-pangs now."

Another member of the family was giving his attention to the fowls. He was earnestly thrusting cake through the wire for their entertainment. When he dropped a piece he picked it up and put it into his own mouth, as though it had been rendered unfit for poultry's consumption. His elders appeared to view his attitude either in indifference or sympathy.

"What are death-pangs like?" said Henry, in another tone.

"I don't know," said his sister, keeping her eyes from the sufferer of them. "And I don't think the hen is having them. It seems not to know anything."

Henry was a tall, solid boy of eight, with rough, dark hair, pale, wide eyes, formless, infantine features, and something vulnerable about him that seemed inconsistent with himself. His sister, a year younger and smaller for her age, had narrower, deeper eyes, a regular, oval face, sudden, nervous movements, and something resistant in her that was again at variance with what was beneath. Tobias at three had small, dark, busy eyes, a fluffy, colourless head, a face that changed with the weeks and evinced an uncertain charm, and a withdrawn expression consistent with his absorption in his own interests. He was still pushing crumbs through the wire when his shoulder was grasped by a hand above him.

"Wasting your cake on the hens! You know you were to eat it yourself."

Toby continued his task as though unaware of interruption.

"Couldn't one of you others have stopped him?"

The latter also seemed unaware of any break.

"Don't do that," said the nursemaid, seizing Toby's arm so that he dropped the cake. "Didn't you hear me speak?"

Toby still seemed not to do so. He retrieved the cake, took a bite himself and resumed his work.

"Don't eat it now," said Eliza. "Give it all to the hens."

Toby followed the injunction, and she waited until the cake was gone.

"Now if I give you another piece, will you eat it?"

"Can we have another piece too?" said the other children, appearing to notice her for the first time.

She distributed the cake, and Toby turned to the wire, but when she pulled him away, stood eating contentedly.

"Soon be better now," he said, with reference to the hen and his dealings with it.

"It didn't get any cake," said Henry. "The others had it all. They took it and then pecked the sick one. Oh, dear, oh, dear!"

"He did get some," said Toby, looking from face to face for reassurance. "Toby gave it to him."

He turned to inspect the position, which was now that the hens, no longer competing for crumbs, had transferred their activity to their disabled companion.

"Pecking him!" said Toby, moving from foot to foot. "Pecking him when he is ill! Fetch William. Fetch him."

A pleasant, middle-aged man, known as the head gardener by virtue of his once having had subordinates, entered the run and transferred the hen to a separate coop.

"That is better, sir."

"Call Toby 'sir'," said the latter, smiling to himself.

"She will be by herself now."

"Sir," supplied Toby.

"Will it get well?" said Henry.

"I can't say, sir."

"Henry and Toby both 'sir'," said Toby. "Megan too."

"No, I am not," said his sister.

"Poor Megan, not 'sir'!" said Toby, sadly.

"The last hen that was ill was put in a coop to die," said Henry, resuming his seat and the mood it seemed to engender in him.

"Well, it died after it was there," said Megan.

"That is better, miss," said William.

"Miss," said Toby, in a quiet, complex tone.

"They go away alone to die," said Henry. "All birds do that, and a hen is a bird. But it can't when it is shut in a coop. It can't act according to its nature."

"Perhaps it ought not to do a thing that ends in dying," said Megan.

"Something in that, miss," said William.

"Why do you stay by the fowls," said Eliza, "when there is the garden for you to play in?"

"We are only allowed to play in part of it," said Henry, as though giving an explanation.

"Oh, dear, oh, dear!" said Eliza, in perfunctory mimicry.

"William forgot to let out the hens," said Megan, "and Toby would not leave them."

Toby tried to propel some cake to the hen in the coop, failed and stood absorbed in the scramble of the others for it.

"All want one little crumb. Poor hens!"

"What did I tell you?" said Eliza, again grasping his arm.

He pulled it away and openly applied himself to inserting cake between the wires.

"Toby not eat it now," he said in a dutiful tone.

"A good thing he does not have all his meals here," said William.

"There is trouble wherever he has them," said Eliza. "And the end is waste."

The sick hen roused to life and flung itself against the coop in a frenzy to join the feast.

"It will kill itself," said Henry. "No one will let it out."

William did so and the hen rushed forth, cast itself into the fray, staggered and fell.

"It is dead," said Henry, almost before this was the case.

"Poor hen fall down," said Toby, in the tone of one who knew the experience. "But soon be well again."

"Not in this world," said William.

"Sir," said Toby, to himself. "No, miss."

"It won't go to another world," said Henry. "It was ill and pecked in this one, and it won't have any other."

"It was only pecked on its last day," said Megan. "And everything is ill before it dies."

"The last thing it felt was hunger, and that was not satisfied."

"It did not know it would not be. It thought it would."

"It did that, miss," said William. "And it was dead before it knew."

"There was no water in the coop," said Henry, "and sick things are parched with thirst."

"Walking on him," said Toby, in a dubious tone.

"Eliza, the hens are walking on the dead one!" said Megan, in a voice that betrayed her.

"It is in their way, miss," said William, giving a full account of the position.

Megan looked away from the hens, and Henry stood with his eyes on them. Toby let the matter leave his mind, or found that it did so.

"Now what is all this?" said another voice, as the head nurse appeared on the scene, and was led by some instinct to turn her eyes at once on Megan. "What is the matter with you all?"

"One of the hens has died," said Eliza, in rapid summary. "Toby has given them his cake and hardly taken a

8

mouthful. The other hens walked on the dead one and upset Miss Megan. Master Henry has one of his moods."

Megan turned aside with a covert glance at William.

"Seeing the truth about things isn't a mood," said Henry.

"It all comes of playing in the wrong place," said Miss Bennet. "You should watch the hens in the field."

"How can we, when they are not there?"

"You know they are there as a rule."

"Very nice place to-day," said Toby, who had heard with a lifted face and a belief that the arrangement was for his convenience. "All together in a large cage."

"Well, it has been a treat for you," said Eliza.

"Because very good boy," said Toby, in a tone of supplying an omission.

"A strange kind of treat," said Henry. "A hen pecked to death, and hungry and thirsty at the last."

"Hens don't mind dying; they die too easily," said Bennet, with conviction in her tone, if nowhere else.

"It was worse than being pecked to death. It was pecked when it was dying."

"They always do that, sir," said William, as if the frequency were a ground for cheer.

Toby stood with his eyes on the dead hen.

"William put him in a cage by himself."

William carried the hen away, smoothing its feathers as he did so.

"William stroke him," said Toby, with approval.

"The hen didn't know about it," said Henry.

"He did know," said Toby.

"It couldn't when it was dead."

"So William stroke him," said Toby. "Poor hen! Toby saw him know."

William resumed his work, and Toby applied himself to attendance upon him, a duty that made consistent inroads upon his time. When William signified his need of a tool, he fetched it with a light on his face and his tongue

9

protruding, and thrust its prongs towards William in earnest co-operation.

"What should I do without you, sir, now that I have no boy?"

"William have one now. Not Henry."

"You grow such a big lad, sir."

"Not lad," said Toby, with a wail in his tone.

"Such a big boy, sir."

"As big as Henry. Just the same. No, the same as Megan," said Toby, ending on an affectionate note.

"Shall I help William?" said Henry, getting off his log.

"No, Toby help him. To-day and to-morrow."

"Isn't it time for your sleep, sir?"

Toby flickered his eyes over Eliza and Bennet, and smoothly resumed his employment.

The latter were engaged in talk so earnest that it might have been assumed to relate to their own affairs. Their interest was given to the family to whom they gave everything. In Bennet's case it was permanent, and in Eliza's susceptible of change. Megan sometimes listened to them; Henry had not thought of doing so; and Toby heard their voices as he heard the other sounds about him.

Eliza was a country girl of twenty-six, with the fairness that results in eyes and brows and lashes of a similar pallor, and features that seem to fail to separate themselves from each other. She had an uneducated expression and an air of knowledge of life that seemed its natural accompaniment. Bennet was a small, spare woman of forty-five, with a thin, sallow face marked by simple lines of benevolence, long, narrow features and large, full eyes of the colour that is called grey because it is no other. She took little interest in herself, and so much in other people that it tended to absorb her being. When the children recalled her to their world, she would return as if from another. They loved her not as themselves, but as the person who served their love of themselves, and greater love has no child than this. She came of tradesman stock and had no need to earn her bread, but consorted with anyone in the house who shared her zest for personal affairs.

"Good-morning, Miss Bennet," said another voice. "Good-morning, Megan. Good-morning, Henry. Is Toby coming to say good-morning to-day?"

"No," said Toby, in an incidental tone.

"Good-morning, ma'am," said Eliza.

"Good-morning, Eliza," said the governess, with a fuller enunciation that she had omitted the greeting before.

"Have you said good-morning to Miss Ridley?" said Bennet.

"Enough people have said it," said Henry, "and the others did not say it to you."

Bennet did not comment on the omission, indeed had not been struck by it, and the two boys who accompanied Miss Ridley did not seem aware of what passed.

"Well, what a beautiful day!" said Miss Ridley.

"It is the same as any other day," said Henry, raising his eyes for his first inspection of it. "Though not for the hen."

"A hen has died and upset them," said Bennet, in a low, confidential tone that the children heard and found comforting. "It will soon pass off."

"Not for the hen," said Henry. "It won't have any day at all."

"We do not quite know that," said Miss Ridley. "Opinions vary on the difference between the animal world and our own."

"Opinions are not much good when no one has the same," said Megan. "They don't tell you anything."

"That again is not quite true. Many people have the same. There are different schools of thought, and people belong to all of them."

"How do you know which to choose?"

"That may be beyond your range. It takes us rather deep."

"What is the good of knowing things, when you have to

get older and older and die before you know everything?"

"You will certainly do that, Megan, and so shall I."

"Are animals of the same nature as we are?" said Henry. "Monkeys look as if they were."

"Yes, that is the line of the truth. A scientist called Darwin has told us about it. Of course we have developed much further."

"Then weren't we made all at once as we are?" said Megan. "Eliza says that would mean the Bible was not true."

"It has its essential truth, and that is what matters."

"I suppose any untrue thing might have that. I daresay a good many have. So there is no such thing as truth. It is different in different minds."

"Why, you will be a philosopher one day, Megan."

Miss Ridley was forty-seven and looked exactly that age. She wore neat, strong clothes that bore no affinity to those in current use, and wore, or had set on her head, an old, best hat in place of a modern, ordinary one. She was fully gloved and booted for her hour in the garden. Her full, pale face, small, steady eyes, nondescript features and confident movements combined with her clothes to make a whole that conformed to nothing and offended no one. She made no mistakes in her dress, merely carried out her intentions.

The two boys who were with her wore rather childish clothes to conform with Henry's. Fabian at thirteen had a broad face and brow, broad, clear features and pure grey eyes that recalled his sister's. Guy was two years younger and unlike him, with a childish, pretty face, dark eyes that might have recalled Toby's, but for their lack of independence and purpose, and a habit of looking at his brother in trust and emulation.

"Well, here are the five of you together," said Miss Ridley, who often made statements that were accepted. "Are you going to have a game before luncheon? It is twelve o'clock."

"That would mean that we amused the younger ones," said Fabian.

"And is there so much objection to that?"

"To me there is too much."

Henry and Megan showed no interest in the enterprise, and Guy looked as if he were not averse from it. Toby, at the mention of the time, had turned and disappeared into some bushes behind him. Eliza went in pursuit, and naturally gained in the contest, as she did her best in it. Toby glanced back to measure her advance, stumbled and fell and lay outstretched and still, uttering despairing cries. His brothers did not look in his direction, and his sister did no more than this. Bennet waited until he emerged in Eliza's arms, his lamentations complicated by his further prospects, and reassured by what she saw, entered into talk with Miss Ridley.

"Have you seen anyone this morning?" she said, in a tone at once eager and casual.

"Mrs. Clare came in to ask about the children. She takes an equal interest in them all. And the tutor came and went. Guy does not do too well with him. I think he is nervous."

Bennet turned eyes of concern on Guy. She had reared the five from the first and saw the infant in all of them.

"Have Mr. and Mrs. Clare been together this morning?"

"Yes, for a time, but old Mr. Clare was with them."

"And that prevented trouble?" said Fabian.

"Why, what trouble should there be?" said Miss Ridley.

"There should not be any, but there would have been. You know what has happened."

"Why, things happen every day, Fabian."

"This has not happened for nine years. My own mother has returned to the place. You must know that."

"Well, I believe I had heard something about it."

"You are right in your belief, as it is likely you would be. You would hardly be the only person not to hear."

"It is nothing for you to think about," said Bennet, in an easy tone that was belied by her eyes.

"It is the only thing. What would anyone think about in our place?"

"You have your mother here."

"We have our stepmother."

"What is a real mother like?" said Guy.

"Like Mater to her own children," said his brother.

"You know that no difference is made," said Miss Ridley.

"The difference is there. There is no need to make it."

"Are all fathers like our father?" said Guy.

"No father is like him," said Fabian. "We have no normal parent."

"He is devoted to you in his way," said Miss Ridley.

"I daresay a cat does the right thing to a mouse in its way."

"Doing things in your own way is not really doing them," said Megan.

"Why, Fabian, what a conscious way of talking!" said Miss Ridley. "And it leads the others to copy you."

"Why should I talk like a child, when my life prevents me from being one?"

"Would having a real mother make us more childish?" said Guy.

"That would hardly be desirable in your case," said Miss Ridley. "You are inclined to be behind your age. And you could not have a stepmother who was more like a real mother."

"And we could not have one who *was* like one," said Fabian.

"You know that every effort is made for you."

"Of course we know. Everyone is at pains to tell us. And we can see it being made, as they can."

"Suppose it was not made? That would be the thing to mind."

"But perhaps not to mind so much."

"Oh, dear, oh, dear!" said Henry.

"Whatever is it?" said Miss Ridley.

"They haven't anything," said Henry, indicating his brothers. "Not even as much as we have."

"Now really you are ungrateful children. You have a beautiful home and every care and kindness. It would do you good to have to face some real trouble."

"You know it would do us harm," said Henry.

"I cannot think what has come over you."

"Then you cannot think at all," said Fabian. "But I daresay that is the case. A good many people can't."

Guy and Megan laughed.

"And you are one of the fortunate ones who can?" said Miss Ridley, using a dry tone.

"I am one of the unfortunate ones who do. That is how I should put it."

"It is perhaps rather a bold claim."

"It is not a claim. It is merely a statement of fact."

"If you know things, of course you think about them," said Megan. "Or you wouldn't really know them."

"You should not say these things before the little ones," said Miss Ridley to Fabian. "Especially if you are a person who thinks. Or do you not think about them?"

"Why should I? They have enough people to do it."

"Henry, do get up from that log," said Bennet, giving matters a lighter tone. "What an uncomfortable seat!"

"Not enough to make you forget anything," said Henry, as if it had failed in its purpose.

"Have we had to bear more than other children?" said Guy. "I mean Fabian and me."

"Now what have you had to bear?" said Miss Ridley. "Try to tell me one thing."

"He doesn't mean hunger and cold like children in books," said Henry. "But they are not the only things."

"Why are Sunday books sadder than others?" said Megan. "It seems to be making it the worst day on purpose. And it is supposed to be the best."

"Now do you not find it so?" said Miss Ridley.

"Only because it is a holiday. Any other day would be better."

"It need not be worse than other days," said Fabian. "The reasons are man-made. Our religion is a gloomy one. There are other and happier creeds."

"Oh, hush, you know there is the one true one," said Bennet, in an automatic manner, not moving her eyes.

"It is a pity it is so sad," said Guy. "It has to mean that life is sad, when religion goes through life."

"Now surely you can think of something pleasant," said Miss Ridley.

"You admit that religion is not that," said Fabian.

"Now I knew you would take me up on that, Fabian. I knew it the moment the words were out of my mouth. Of course it has its solemn side. Its very depth and meaning involve that. We should not wish it otherwise."

"Well, people do like gloom. It prevents other people from being happy."

"But surely they do not wish that."

"They seem to go through life wishing it. They think happiness is wrong."

"Or they think it is too pleasant," said Megan, "and so don't want other people to have it."

"My dear child, what reason can you have for saying such a thing?"

"That I am not one of those who have eyes and see not, ears and hear not, and seeing do not perceive," said Megan, twisting round on one leg.

"I am afraid you are conceited children."

"Everyone is conceited. It is only that some people pretend not to be. People can't always despise themselves, and there might not be any reason."

"I daresay they could generally find one," said Fabian.

"If they want to prevent people's happiness, they certainly could," said Miss Ridley.

"Miss Ridley is conceited," said Henry, in an expressionless tone.

"What am I conceited about, Henry?"

"About your brain and your learning."

"I wonder if I am," said Miss Ridley, consenting to turn attention to herself. "I hardly think so, Henry. About my brain I certainly am not. It is of the strong and useful kind, but no more. In learning I have gone further than I expected."

Miss Ridley had obtained a degree, a step whose mystic significance for a woman was accepted at that date even by those who had taken it. It rendered her equal to the instruction of male youth, and accounted for her presence in the family.

Eliza came towards them, calling out to Bennet tidings that were worth announcing from afar.

"He was asleep in a minute. He was fractious because he was tired."

"Dear little boy!" said Miss Ridley.

"Is there anything endearing in being asleep?" said Fabian. "Not that it is not better than screaming on the ground."

"People are always glad when babies go to sleep," said Henry. "They can stop thinking about them. They take too much thought."

"You don't deserve to have a baby brother," said Miss Ridley.

"Well, we did not want one."

"I remember how excited you were when he came."

"But not when he stayed," said Megan, smiling. "Not when he had always to be there."

"I was never excited at all," said Henry. "I knew he would have to stay. I knew it wouldn't be Megan and me any longer."

"I am afraid that is a selfish point of view."

"All points of view are selfish," said Megan. "They are the way people look at things themselves. So they must be."

17

"Both knees are grazed," said Eliza to Bennet, as though this might have been expected.

"Oh, dear, oh, dear!" said Henry.

"Come, that is not so bad," said Miss Ridley. "Children must sometimes fall, and he was very brave."

"Was he?" said Fabian. "How would cowardice be shown?"

"I wasn't thinking of him," said Henry. "There are other things that matter. And Megan and I don't always think about him. I had a thought of my own."

"You ought to get out of the habit of saying, 'Oh, dear, oh, dear!' "

"It isn't a habit. I don't say it if there isn't a reason. Reasons can't be a habit. They are there."

"You are proud of saying it," said Guy, "because great minds tend to melancholy. I know the book that says it."

"I don't read the book; I don't often read," said Henry.

"Now there is another change we might see," said Miss Ridley.

"There are real changes that ought to be made, and never will be," said Henry, checking his natural exclamation.

"Now there is the first effort made. I congratulate you, Henry."

"I wasn't making an effort."

"I think you were. You see I think better of you than you think of yourself."

"People are always ashamed of trying to be better," said Megan.

"I should be sorry to think so," said Miss Ridley. "Would you be ashamed of it?"

"I shall never know, because I shall never try."

"I think that shows you would be," said Guy.

"Now Henry may say, 'Oh, dear, oh, dear!' " said Miss Ridley. "I see there is reason."

"People are ashamed of thinking they are not good enough as they are," said Fabian.

"And yet they would not admit to a high opinion of themselves," said another voice. "I suppose they could not, as it would be so very high."

"Good-morning, Mrs. Clare," said Miss Ridley. "Say good-morning to your mother, children."

The children smiled without speaking, according to a law which they never broke, and of which their mother was not aware.

"Why do you play just here, the one unpleasant place? Did not one out of half-a-dozen of you think of that?"

"Everyone thought of it," said Megan, "but Toby wanted to watch the hens."

"Did he leave directions that you were all to abide by his choice?"

Megan laughed, and her mother kissed her and turned to the boys.

"How are all my sons this morning? No one in trouble, I hope?" she said, her eyes going to Henry and Guy, who were disposed to this state.

"Some minds tend to it," said Henry, raising his eyes to her face.

"Guy is pale this morning, Miss Ridley. He does not seem as strong as the others."

"He is not, Mrs. Clare. Indeed he is one by himself in many ways."

"And Fabian's clothes look different. The brothers should be alike."

"He is reaching the stage of choice. And likeness to younger brothers is not always part of it."

"Well, if he knows his own mind, he has a right to follow it."

"You are an indulgent mother, Mrs. Clare."

"I never see why children should not please themselves, as long as they do nothing wrong."

"Would it be wrong not to learn anything?" said Henry.

"It would be wrong of me to let you be unprepared for life."

"Toby is unprepared, and people seem to like him."

"Dear little boy! I should hope he is at three years old."

"I ought not to be so very prepared at eight."

"Well, I do not suppose you are, my little son."

"I am more prepared than you know. I am ready for things to happen. Is Megan more prepared than I am?"

"I should not wonder. Little girls sometimes are."

"They are all of the independent type," said Miss Ridley. "Guy is again the exception."

"Fabian and Megan remind me of each other. They are true brother and sister."

"They are really only half one," said Henry.

"You surely do not feel that?"

"No, I just know it," said Henry, as he followed the others.

Flavia Clare looked after the group of children. She was a tall, thin woman of forty, with a wide, full head, a firm, curved mouth, honest hazel eyes that seemed to know their own honesty, and hair and clothes as unadorned and unadorning as custom permitted. An air about her of being a personality suggested that she was aware of this, and was careful to give it no thought.

"It is hard to be impartial to them all, Miss Ridley. I wonder how far I succeed."

"I should say to an unusual degree, Mrs. Clare. I always feel inclined to congratulate you."

"And I gave you the opportunity. What do you think, Miss Bennet? I am giving it to you as well."

"Yes. Oh, yes," said Bennet, recalling her eyes and her thoughts. "People say they might all be your own children."

"And you would not say it? I have tried to make them so."

"You could not do any more," said Bennet, in a tone of honest sympathy.

"And there is so much more to be done. I did not know how much it would be, how easy it would be to fail. But I suppose some failure must be accounted human success. We must be content with our human place."

A bell rang in the house, and Miss Ridley turned and went towards it with a running gait, that seemed to incommode her without adding to her speed. Bennet followed without sign of haste, and they reached the house together. The children went severally to the nursery and the schoolroom, in accordance with the convention that allotted the most stairs to the shortest legs, or to those that had to be spared them.

Bennet sat at the head of her table, with Henry and Megan at the sides. Eliza's place was at the bottom, with Toby's high chair at her hand, so that she could divide her attention between her own meals and his. As she carried him from his bed to the chair, he exhibited signs of revulsion and turned his face over her shoulder.

"Oh, your own nice chair!"

"No," said Toby.

"We don't want anyone else to sit in it."

Toby cast eyes of suspicion on Henry and Megan, and Eliza took advantage of the moment to insert him into the chair. He bowed to fate to the extent of merely uttering fretting sounds.

"Now look at the nice dinner," said Eliza.

Toby gave it a glance of careless appraisement and settled to a game with his bib and mug, that involved a crooning song. When a spoon approached his lips he shut them tight.

"Now what about feeding yourself?" said Eliza, in a zestful manner.

Toby took the spoon, misled by the tone, but was repelled by the routine and cast the spoon on the ground. Eliza took another without a change of expression and proceeded to feed him, and he presently leaned over the chair.

"Poor spoon!" he said.

"Yes, poor spoon! You have thrown it on the floor. It is all by itself down there."

"Oh, yes. All by itself. Toby not throw it. Eliza did."

"No, no, you know quite well you threw it yourself. Now eat your dinner or you won't be a good boy," said Eliza, accepting Toby's moral range.

A look of consternation came into the latter's eyes, and he ate industriously.

"Very good boy," he said, appealing to Bennet.

"Yes, if you eat your dinner."

Toby returned to his plate, but misliking the scraps left upon it, took it in both hands and threw it after the spoon. It broke and he fell into mirth.

"Dear, dear, what a naughty thing to do!" said Eliza.

Toby was lost in his emotion.

Henry and Megan picked up the pieces and broke them, to divert him further. The method succeeded too well, and he showed signs of hysteria and exhaustion.

"No, no, go back to your seats," said Bennet. "He will be upset."

Henry threw down the last fragment, and Toby's mirth brought a look of perplexity to his own face as to its pleasurable nature.

"Now look at the plate all in pieces," said Eliza. "It was unkind of Toby."

"It likes it," said the latter after a moment's inspection. "Only one plate. Now three, five, sixteen."

"No, it does not like it. How would Toby like to be broken?"

"Toby little boy."

"Will he eat that pudding?" said Bennet. "It will be safer not to try."

"After all that," said Eliza.

Toby looked up in a frowning manner, and after a minute of watching the pudding disappear, made signs of peremptory demand. He was given a portion and ate it without help, scraping his plate and setting down his spoon with precision. Then he gave a reminiscent giggle.

"Another plate."

"You have one in front of you," said Henry.

"Oh, no," said Toby.

"You are a good boy not to throw it," said Eliza.

"Not throw it. Oh, no. Poor plate."

"You are too big to be so naughty," said Bennet to Henry. "Toby sets you an example."

"You always tell us to amuse him," said Megan, "and nothing has ever amused him so much."

"Amuse him," said Toby. "Toby laugh, didn't he?"

"Why did he think it was so funny?" said Megan.

Toby looked up as if interested in the response.

"He has a sense of humour like a savage," said Henry.

"No," said his brother.

"Savages laugh when the others' heads are blown off, even when their own are just going to be. Their minds are like Toby's."

"Or like yours, when you told him about the plate," said Eliza, with simply disparaging intent.

"Henry," said Toby, in agreement with this criticism. "Dear Toby!"

"Now you must be ready to go downstairs," said Bennet, rising and laying hands on Megan.

"Can't we send down word that I am not very well?"

Bennet continued her ministrations without reply.

"Dear Toby!" said the latter, leaning towards Bennet in insistence on this point of view.

"Yes, yes, dear Toby!"

Toby relapsed into his own pursuits, and wrapping his bib round his mug, rocked it to and fro.

"The mug would break, if you threw it down," said Henry.

Toby raised a warning finger and hushed the mug in his arms.

CHAPTER II

"ANOTHER MEAL!" said Cassius Clare, coming to the luncheon table. "The same faces, the same voices, the same things said. I daresay the same food."

"You should provide another voice and face," said his father. "You set the example of always bringing your own."

"I wonder if we could dispense with meals," said Cassius, using a sincere tone.

"And what is your conclusion?"

"We might perhaps dispense with luncheon. The children have it upstairs, and older people do not need so much to eat."

"Any arrangement you wish could be made in your case."

"Perhaps you are too old to go so long without food."

"I could have a tray in my room. That would be in accordance with my age."

"And then there would only be your own face," said Flavia, "and I suppose no voice."

"And Flavia might say she wanted something to eat in the middle of the day," said Cassius.

"It is true that I might," said his wife.

"So it only leaves me to dispense with the meal. And that would not make much difference."

"It would to yourself," said old Mr. Clare. "Have you thought of the difference it would make?"

"It may not be worth while to make the change for one person."

"It is for you to decide," said Flavia. "It involves no one else."

"So you have upset your scheme, my boy," said Mr. Clare.

Cassius began to carve the meat, breathing rather deeply.

"Will you have any of this?" he said to his wife.

"I will have what I usually do."

"A good deal, isn't it?" said Cassius, seeming to operate with some effort.

"I should think an average amount."

"This is not a meal we were to dispense with," said Mr. Clare.

"I think most women eat less," said Cassius, looking at the plate as it left him.

"Well, this is what I will eat," said his wife.

"I wonder what we are quarrelling about."

"You can hardly do that, my boy, as you have arranged it," said Mr. Clare.

"Do you think that bookcase would look better further to the left?" said Cassius, with his head to one side.

"Not to me, when I have seen it where it is for so long. It would look in the wrong place. And I should think it would to you, as you have seen it there for even longer."

Cassius regarded it in independent consideration.

"Did you say you had seen the children this morning?" he said to his wife, as though realising no more than this about her utterance.

"I did not say so, as you know. But I have seen them or seen four of them," said Flavia, her voice changing as she spoke. "And a picture they made, alike and different, and individual and the same. Toby was still asleep."

"Did Miss Ridley add to the picture?"

"She looked herself, as she does. Yes, she added something of her own. I hope the post is what she needs."

"I hope she is the person to fill it. That should be our concern."

"It was naturally our chief one. It should not exclude the other. I am afraid it tends to do so."

"I am sure of it," said Mr. Clare. "I would not say I was afraid."

Cassius looked at his companions' plates, and took a

shred of meat himself, as if to fill the time. In a moment he gave a sigh and fully supplied his plate, as though conformity were unavoidable. As he did so, he happened to meet his wife's eyes.

"Having my luncheon after all!" he said, as if quoting her thought.

"A good many people are doing that."

"But they did not say they would not have any," said Cassius, still in the quoting tone.

"I daresay they did. It is a thing people do."

"So I am just like anyone else?"

"No, you need not be afraid of it, my boy," said Mr. Clare.

"Like a good many people in that," said Flavia.

"And you are different?" said Cassius.

"I may be in the minority. The matter is a small one."

"How many of us think that about ourselves?"

"All of us," said his father. "And not only on that ground."

"On more important ones?"

"Yes, yes, on those, my boy."

"I hardly think we are all so much alike," said Flavia.

"Neither do I," said Cassius. "I often wonder if I belong to the same species as other people."

"And what conclusion do you come to?" said Mr. Clare.

"To my own conclusion. I daresay you often wonder it about yourself."

"No, I know I belong to the same. I have had long enough to learn it."

"Do we mean the same thing, or not?"

"The same," said Flavia, smiling. "Everyone always means it."

"Now there is something I have been wanting to say," said Cassius, replenishing his plate, as if his thoughts were elsewhere. "Fabian is getting too old to be with women and children."

"He will go to a public school in a year. A home life is

26

best for boys in childhood. It is what I shall do for Henry, and so what I do for his brothers."

"I suppose Guy is your favourite of your stepchildren?"

"I have no stepchildren. I have four sons and a daughter. I can see it in no other way."

"I wonder if they can," said Cassius.

"If so, the blame is mine."

"Their opinion of you would hardly be the same as your opinion of yourself."

"Then perhaps the blame is theirs," said Mr. Clare. "Children are not always blameless."

"I wonder if they ought to see their own mother," said Cassius, keeping his tone even. "You know she has returned to the place?"

"Yes, I know," said his wife.

"I am not a man who cannot change his mind."

"It seems that you are not."

"The best way to deal with a mistake is to rectify it."

"If a mistake has been made."

"It is never too late to mend."

"A poor saying," said Mr. Clare.

"Not to mend ourselves," said Flavia. "To mend what we have done, it is often too late. I think it generally is."

"Do you feel with me that we took a wrong course?" said Cassius.

"No, I think we did the best thing. I do not say there was any good thing."

"No mistake was made at the time," said Mr. Clare. "None could have been made."

"A man's feelings may change," said his son, not looking at anyone.

"You need not tell us, my boy. You give us the proof."

"They have a way of returning," said Flavia, "with the return of the things that caused them. Just as they pass with their passing."

"You think you are very wise and deep," said her husband.

"Well, it sounded as if she was," said Mr. Clare.

"And the words suggested it to Cassius," said Flavia, "and he is not prone to such opinion."

"One woman and two men!" said Cassius, as if to himself. "I suppose this is what it must be."

"And would a second woman mend matters?" said his wife. "Well, perhaps she might. She might be the right person in the right place, doing the thing she could do."

"My dear, good wife!" said Cassius, in another and louder tone. "My helpmeet in the troubles of life! How I depend on you in my mind, if I have my own ways of showing it! I know you understand me."

"Well, that is fortunate," said his father. "It might not be so."

"I want your advice, Flavia. I ask for it, my dear. Would you advise me to approach my first wife? Your opinion will be mine."

"I hardly know what my opinion is. I have not thought. I should not think. It has no bearing on the matter."

"Ah, I have never met a little woman with such an opinion of herself. Or one with a better right to it. But why not help a simple man in his own way? Unless you are afraid of what is in your mind. I daresay we all are really."

"Oh, well, afraid of that. But we should not betray it. We always take great care."

"To involve other people and protect ourselves?"

"Well, think what care that would need."

"The thing to do is to keep it in our minds and to continue to be afraid of it," said Mr. Clare.

"Well, what else could we do?" said his daughter-in-law. "There is no danger that we shall accustom ourselves to it. It is not true that we get used to anything."

"You both talk as if you had dark thoughts on a heroic scale," said Cassius, as if this were a too ambitious claim.

"Just on the ordinary scale," said his wife.

"Now here is a letter come by hand," said Cassius. "And

I declare the one I dreaded! I might have known it. I expect I did know in my mind, and that is what put me into such a state. Well, what a thing to confront a man in the first half of the day, and cast a cloud over the rest of it!"

"Letters usually come at breakfast," said his father. "And then the effect might be on the whole day."

"And that is helpful, is it? And common is the commonplace, and empty chaff well meant for grain. That things are common would not make my own less bitter. Never morning wore to evening but something of the kind took place."

"It does sound rather like the whole day," said Flavia.

"Yes, you can be clever about it. How does that affect the position?"

"I think it improves it a little. What does the letter say?"

"Read it to us, my boy," said Mr. Clare.

"Oh, yes, and have you and Flavia throwing your wit over it, and treating me as if I were a culprit, instead of a man expected to be married to two wives at once, and to offer up one of them to the mockery of the other. What a demand to be made on a man! I could not have believed it."

"I do not believe it," said his wife.

"Come, you can be explicit, my boy," said Mr. Clare.

"I am putting it as plainly as I can. Surely two wives is explicit enough for anyone. Or would you want it to be ten? Would that be more explicit?"

"No, it would be less," said Flavia. "It would need a good deal more explanation."

"Well, have the truth," said her husband. "Have it and make what you can of it. Here am I told by my first wife that she is coming to encounter my second, and to break up our family life, and take our children away from us, and be a heroine and a martyr through it all! Though she does not want to see me. Oh, no, there is no mention of that. Though what harm it would do her I am at a loss to say. She did it day and night for five years."

"And felt she could do it no longer," said Flavia, in an expressionless tone.

"And I felt the same, I can tell you, and felt it no less. To have those eyes boring straight into mine, as if they would read my very soul, and probably find I hadn't one into the bargain! It was as much as flesh and blood could stand. I had come to an end as much as she had."

"Is she returning to the place for good?" said Mr. Clare.

"Coming back to her home, as she puts it," said Cassius, referring to the letter. "As if this house had not been her home for years! There is no need to be invidious, is there? Coming back to that brother and sister, and to that house with books all over it, and little else that I could ever see. Well, if she prefers it to this, I wish her joy of it."

"She hardly has the choice of the two," said his father. "And she has come with a purpose and told you of it."

"Oh, yes, she wants something for herself. There is no need to say that."

"I should not have thought it need be said of her, from what I have heard," said Flavia.

"Yes, be magnanimous about her. We know your view of yourself."

"It is the way to make it everyone's view of her," said Mr. Clare. "And there is no harm in her taking it."

"Yes, I am the one who is criticised and condemned, and seen as a common creature blundering between two highminded women, and inflicting myself on both. That is my position. I must put up with it."

"What is it that your first wife wants for herself?" said Flavia.

"Oh, I thought you said she would not want anything."

"But you did not take that view."

"And I do not take it," said Cassius. "She seems to me to want all she can get, as in her way she always did. She and I parted by mutual consent, but no one was to know that but ourselves. Oh, no, she was the martyr and I the culprit, and the world had to see it like that. And now she thinks she can call the tune, as if it were the truth. It is a thing that makes my blood boil."

Cassius was a broad, solid man about fifty, with a broad, fair face, small, light eyes, thick, uncertain hands, and flat, not uncomely features, that responded to his emotions. His father, who was like him, had a stronger growth of bone, that raised and strengthened his features to the point of handsomeness. Flavia looked a creature of another blood between them. She seemed to watch her husband, while her father-in-law simply accepted him. Mr. Clare saw his son as he was, and kept his feeling for him, and Flavia seemed to fear to do the one, in case she should cease to do the other.

Cassius was the master of the place, which he had inherited from a godfather, and Mr. Clare on the death of his wife had joined his fortunes with his son's.

"Read the letter to us, my boy. Then we shall know our ground."

" 'Dear Cassius,' " read his son, in a voice that challenged them to form their own opinion, " 'I am breaking my word. I have not strength to keep it. I cannot be parted longer from my sons. It is not in me to suffer it. I am coming back to my home. I must be within daily distance of them. Indeed I have come back. I ask you to allow me access to them. If you will not, I shall still seek it. I do not ask for forgiveness. I see there can and could be none. I do not ask for what is beyond people's power. I am the last person who should do that. Catherine Clare.'

"There is a letter for you. What do you think of that as a threat to our lives? Catherine sneaking in and out of our home, and none of us knowing whether to accept her or not! And an atmosphere of discomfort and uncertainty over everything."

"She would hardly do that," said Flavia. "I know her only by hearsay, but enough to know that."

"Yes, stand up for her. Put yourself in her place. I might have foreseen this. Two women against one man, when two men against one woman would be the better match! And two mothers for those boys! What a state of things!"

"I hope both mothers will be real ones. And I see no reason why they should not."

"Well, I do. From what I know of you both I see no hope of it. Oh, I am not a stranger to either of you. And I don't see you working together, and there is the truth."

"There should not be any problem, if there is goodwill on both sides. And there is no reason against it."

"No reason? Well, you are a simpler woman than I thought you. So you can honestly say that. Well, I believe you are simpler. I believe you put a veneer on yourself and deceive us all. I believe people often do that."

"It is an example that might be followed," said Mr. Clare.

"Your willingness to let her see the boys puts the matter on its foundation," said Flavia.

"My willingness? Who said I was willing? I tell you I am not. I don't want to have her in my home, looking as if she would penetrate into the heart of things, and as if she were too sensitive to look at them when she had done so. Oh, she has her own view of herself. Just as you have, for the matter of that. Women think much more of themselves than men."

"Well, that does no harm," said Mr. Clare, "if it leads them to live up to it."

"Well, it casts an atmosphere of falseness and consciousness over everything," said Cassius, in an easier tone. "And now I suppose I am to answer this letter. And say—well, say what I can. Just to accept what she says would make me cut a poor figure. Or is that what I am to do? Can't either of you utter a word, or have a thought, or give me any kind of help? What is the good of feminine insight and the experience of seventy years, if they can't be turned to account?"

"You have only to write what is in your mind," said his wife.

"I have told you what that is. So I am to write that, am I? Well, I will do so and let you see the result," said Cassius rising with an air of reckless purpose.

"Why be in such a hurry, my boy?" said his father. "It is not a case for eagerness."

"Eagerness? No, it is not. So I will do nothing and see what comes of that. Though I have not much hope that the matter will rest there. I know the woman I am dealing with."

Cassius took a deep breath as his wife and his father left him, and then squared his shoulders and addressed the butler, who had been waiting on them, or ostensibly doing so.

"Well, Ainger, have you gained an idea of my position?"

"I have caught a word here and there, sir," said Ainger, looking up in an incidental manner.

"You remember your former mistress?"

"Five years of my life were spent under her sway, sir. It can hardly have escaped me."

"She is returning to my life after nine years, or that is the suggestion."

"I did not gather your decision, sir," said Ainger, contracting his brows as in an effort of recollection.

"I have no choice in the matter. It is out of my control."

"It seems that a mother's feelings command respect, sir."

"So you heard the whole thing. I thought you did."

"It recurs to me, sir, as an undercurrent to my work, as I cast my mind over it."

Alfred Ainger was a tall, active man of forty, with a round, yellow head, a full, high-coloured face, very blue, bunched-up eyes, an unshapely nose and a red-lipped, elaborate mouth that opened and shut with a vigorous movement. His bearing carried an equal respect for his master and confidence in himself.

"Well, you may soon be opening the door to your former mistress."

"I shall know what is required of me, sir."

"I hope I may say the same, Ainger. I hope I shall be able to support one wife and receive the other, and do a man's part by both."

"The young gentlemen should be a help to you, sir."

"Yes, it is they whom she is coming to see. I do not flatter myself it is anyone else. I do not wish to do so. But I shall have to meet the several claims and forget my own. I hope I shall be equal to it."

CHAPTER III

Bᴇɴɴᴇᴛ sᴇᴛ Toʙʏ down at the dining-room door and constrained her charges to enter. They advanced and stood about the table, as seats for them were not supplied. Toby went on to the window-seat, disposed some playthings upon it and entered into communication with them.

"Is my baby coming to his mother?" said Flavia. "I have not seen him to-day."

Toby said nothing except to his possessions.

"Come and have a word with your grandfather," said Mr. Clare.

Toby paused for a moment and then ran towards him and displayed his knees.

"You have grazed the pair of them. So you had a fall."

"Henry push him," said Toby, in a tone of suggestion.

"No, he did not," said Megan. "Toby fell when Eliza ran after him to take him to bed."

"Run fast," said her brother. "Toby too."

"We should say what is true," said Flavia, stroking his head.

"A plate," said Toby, with a giggle, looking round the table.

"A plate was broken and made him laugh," said Henry. "He can still be happy easily."

"Oh, dear! Who broke it?" said Flavia.

"Eliza did," said Toby, soberly.

"No, he broke it himself," said Megan. "He threw it on the ground."

"You must know that you broke it," said Flavia to Toby. "And poor Eliza, who is always so kind!"

"Oh, yes. Very kind. Not mean to run too fast."

"Suppose she said what was not true about you?"

"No," said Toby, on a note of protest.

"Did you not know when you broke the plate?"

"Very good boy," said Toby, in a tone of taking precaution before admission.

"Yes, if you say what is true. Say you broke the plate yourself."

"Oh, yes," said Toby solemnly. "Throw it down. Poor plate!"

He returned to the window and resumed his monologue.

"Does he often say what is not true?" said Cassius.

"He doesn't know that words are connected with truth," said Fabian. "He is confused by having stories told him."

"Nothing must be told him but actual facts. I have wondered if tales should be told to young children. And here is the answer."

"It would not be natural," said his son. "And it would not make any difference. The infant mind invents stories. All infancy is the same. In the infancy of the race tales were invented."

"Have we been wrong in deciding on a home education?" said Flavia, smiling at her husband.

Cassius made no reply.

"Toby doesn't know that things as they are, are all there is," said Henry. "He can still believe anything and be happy."

"And your knowledge of life is too much for you?" said his father.

"It must get more and more. How can it be helped?"

"You were the hero of one of Toby's inventions," said Mr. Clare. "Does fiction owe anything to fact?"

Henry did not reply.

"Answer your grandfather," said Cassius.

Henry was silent.

"Flavia, will you support me?"

"No, all the children are good to Toby. Henry knows it goes without saying."

"I admit I had not studied them," said Mr. Clare.

36

"Well, you have been told now," said Henry.

"I am glad you have found your tongue," said his father, as if he had carried his point.

"Toby knows what is possible," said Guy. "That is why his stories might be true. He has got to know much more in the last months."

"My observant son!" said Flavia.

"That is true of all children," said Cassius.

"I meant more than that," said Guy. "He keeps seeming to be a different person."

"You might emulate him," said his father.

"Guy is too old to change like that," said Fabian.

"He is perhaps too old not to have changed."

"There is no rule in these things," said Flavia. "They will all come into their own."

"I think the elder ones are the higher type," said Cassius, in an even tone. "Especially if Guy's backwardness is a passing phase."

"Well, their mother is a gifted woman. I have heard many people say so. It is natural that her children should take after her."

"Has she more gifts than you have?" said Henry.

"Yes, I think she probably has."

"Do children inherit only from mothers?"

"No, from both their parents."

"Then Father might have some gifts for us to inherit."

"He hardly seems to think you have inherited any."

"Sometimes stocks do not mix," said Cassius, putting his hand to his boot and giving it a pull. "A union may not result in the best in either."

"It seems a pity," said Megan, "that when two women agreed to marry Father, he did not like being married to either of them."

"He liked being married to both of them at first," said Flavia, leaning towards her and including all the children with her eyes. "He had real happiness with each. And he and I are often happy together now. But time must bring changes. It cannot be helped or explained."

"It could be explained, I expect," said her daughter, "if people liked to do it. I daresay most things could be. But I see they would not like to."

"How would you manage it?" said Cassius.

"I did not mean I was different from other people."

"What is the good of anything, if nothing lasts?" said Henry.

"One thing lasts," said Flavia, bending forward. "A mother's love for her children."

"And they haven't their mother," said Henry, looking at his brothers. "And she hasn't them, even though her love lasts. Oh, dear, oh, dear!"

"They share your mother with you."

"The boy must see what is before him," said Cassius.

"Everyone has to do that," said his son.

"Oh, dear, oh, dear!" said Cassius.

"Yes, that is what it is, though people don't understand it."

"Mater's little boy," said Toby, running across the room.

"Yes, that is what you are," said Flavia.

Toby rested his eyes on Henry, and his mother misinterpreted him.

"Yes, Mater's two little boys."

"No," said Toby, with a wail.

"No, it is only Toby."

"Not Megan," said Toby, waited for assurance and returned to his play.

"Is no one troubled by standing?" said Mr. Clare.

"We never have chairs," said Henry.

"Surely that does not matter for half-an-hour," said his father.

"I did not say it did."

"Did you not imply it? Using that self-pitying tone!"

"We only have one voice to use for everything."

"Yours is certainly used only for one thing. It is useful for that."

"Well, yours is only used for one thing too."

"And what is that?"

"You would not like it, if I told you, and I expect you know."

"Is Miss Ridley waiting for you all?" said Flavia.

"I don't know," said Megan. "Yes, I suppose she is."

"She reads a book," said Guy. "I expect we shall have to go for a walk."

"What an obligation!" said Cassius. "It is almost as bad as being without a chair. Surely Fabian does not walk with women and children?"

"We go with Bennet or Eliza," said Megan. "Only he and Guy go with Miss Ridley."

"An odd sight it must be."

"We are not self-conscious," said Fabian.

"Do you mean that I am?" said his father.

"I did not mean anything, but it sounds as if you must be."

"Do you all like Miss Ridley?" said Mr. Clare.

"I don't mind her, Grandpa," said Megan.

"And the boy, Henry?"

"I don't mind her either."

"Toby not mind her," said Toby, running forward.

"I wonder if she minds any of you," said Flavia, smiling.

"She minds Guy the least," said Henry.

"I think that is a common view of Guy. But I am sure she is kind to you all."

"Bennet is kind," said Toby.

Eliza entered to fetch her charges, and Toby departed on her arm without a backward glance, nursing his possessions. In the schoolroom Miss Ridley, clothed to go out, was reading on an upright chair. She rose, put the marker in her book and carried it with her.

"Now where shall we go for our walk? Whose turn is it to choose?"

"Let us go to the hayfield, where we can sit down," said Guy.

Miss Ridley set off in this direction, looking at the scene about her and drawing her pupils' attention to anything of interest by the way. Her life was divided between her conscience and her inclination; it was her concern to strike the mean between them, and her merit that she did so.

"Now get some exercise," she said, as she took her own seat on some hay.

The boys moved out of her sight and sank down on the ground.

"Walking doesn't seem to have any meaning," said Guy.

"It ought to come under the head of hard labour," said his brother. "As it does in prisons, where the treadmill is a form of it. I wish Henry had not so much sympathy with us. We know we are in a pathetic position."

"Are we?" said Guy, with some interest.

"You are not, because you do not realise you are."

"I know we are not with our own mother."

"I don't think you do. It is Henry who knows. I wish he could forget."

"Boys," called Miss Ridley, her voice revealing that she did not raise her eyes from her book, "you are not idling, are you?"

Her pupils were silent, as though out of earshot, and resumed in a lower tone.

"Our characters are getting worse," said Guy. "I think it is because it does not matter to anyone."

"I should not have expected you to see that."

"I see things more often than I used to. That is what Father does not know."

"You are altering as quickly as Toby," said Fabian, turning on his elbow to look at his brother.

"Has Father ever been fond of anyone?"

"Of both his wives, if the present one is to be believed."

"She is always to be believed," said Guy.

"That is true. So he was fond of both, but failed to maintain the feeling."

"Did our mother go away from him, or he from her?"

"They arranged a divorce. I heard Bennet telling Miss Ridley. She stayed away for years, and now she has come back. Her home was always here, with her brother and sister. It is less than a mile away, and we have not seen her for nine years. It was supposed to be best. I wonder what the worst would have been."

"What should we call her, if we saw her?"

"We called her 'Mother'. I can just remember. That is why we called this mother 'Mater'. And then the younger ones called her the same, so that there should be no difference."

"What is the colour of our mother's hair?"

"It used to be dark, but perhaps it is grey by now. I thought she was tall, but I believe she is not. I wish we could leave this house that has never been a home to us."

"What is a real home like?"

"It is something you do not know, and I can only just remember. My life was over when I was four. I wonder how many people can say that."

"Then I have hardly had a life at all."

"Well, you have accepted a substitute."

"I never know whether I have or not. I don't see how I can know."

"Boys, look at those corncrakes," said Miss Ridley, appearing round the haystack with the effect of something artificial at war with nature. "We do not often see two together. And listen to their raucous cry. It is a sound one always likes to hear."

"It is true that one does," said Fabian, "though there does not seem any reason."

"Have you finished your book?" said Guy.

"Yes, some time ago. I have been enjoying my surroundings. And now we must turn towards home."

"What is the word supposed to mean?" said Fabian.

"Come, come, no more of that," said Miss Ridley.

When they reached the garden, Henry and Megan were standing about it, unoccupied. Toby, who was never in this state, was once more devoted to the service of William, who was shovelling litter into a barrow. Toby was plucking single leaves and adding them to its contents.

"Soon be full," he said to Miss Ridley.

"You are a busy little boy."

"Big boy. So very busy."

"Will you be a gardener when you grow up, sir?" said William.

"No, Toby have one."

"Will you have me, sir?"

"Yes, have William."

"Father has him," said Megan.

"No, not Father; Toby."

"Perhaps Father will be dead by then," said Henry.

"Yes, poor Father."

"What will you be yourself, sir, when you are a man?"

"Have a church," said Toby. "Speak in a loud voice."

"Well, I shall come to your church, sir."

"Oh, no," said Toby instantly. "Not people like William."

"What kind of people?" said Megan.

"People like Father."

"Do you like Father better than William?"

"No, like William."

"You would want everyone to come to your church," said Miss Ridley.

"Oh, no," said Toby, solemnly. "Not church."

"Why do you choose this part of the garden?" said Miss Ridley, not carrying the subject further.

"Toby wanted to talk to William," said Henry.

"But Eliza is watching Toby," said Miss Ridley, perceiving the former standing in the background in fulfilment of her afternoon duty of seeing that Toby's contentment did not fail. "Why don't you find something to do? Toby sets you an example."

"He doesn't understand what William is doing," said Henry.

"William say 'Thank you'," said Toby, in refutation of this.

"Doesn't he ever bring more than one leaf at a time?"

"Oh, no," said Toby, placing a leaf with care. "One little leaf."

William threw a flower-pot into the barrow, and Toby fell into mirth as it broke. William threw another with similar result, and Eliza started forward in consternation.

"He must not get excited at this time of the day."

"Not time for tea," said Toby, with a scowling violence that supported her.

William tossed a dead mole into the barrow.

"No," said Toby, shrilly. "Poor little mouse!"

William displayed the mole in his hand, and Henry came up and gazed at it.

"How soon will decay set in?"

"It has real hands," said Megan.

Toby bent his head and reverently kissed the mole.

"Very soft. Nice fur. Dear little mouse!"

"Why did it die?" said Megan, in an offhand manner.

"Well, everything dies in the end, miss. It will happen to us all."

Megan's face cleared at the thought of this common fate. The mole had only borne what she would bear herself.

"Now you can have a funeral," said Eliza, in simple congratulation.

"We must put the mole in a box," said Henry, with more zest that he had shown that day. "Or it will just enrich the ground as it decays."

"It wouldn't know anything about that," said his sister.

The burial took place later, as preparation was involved. Toby officiated at his own insistence, and Eliza and the other children followed the mole to the grave. William was hailed and his attendance demanded, Toby waiving the question of the class of his congregation in favour of its size.

"So I am at your church after all, sir."

Toby raised a finger and began to speak.

"O dear people, we are gathered together. Dearly beloved brethren. Let us pray. Ashes and ashes. Dust and dust. This is our brother. Poor little mole! Until he rise again. Prayers of the congregation. Amen."

"Why, you will make a proper parson, sir."

Toby took no notice and went on his knees, signing to his audience to follow. William was behindhand in his response, and Toby frowned upon him and waited for it.

"The Lord keep you. His face shine. Kneel down a long time before you go. Give you peace. Amen."

The company rose with a rustle certainly reminiscent of a dispersing congregation, and another voice was heard.

"What is all this? How did he learn this sort of thing? How and when did it happen? I desire to know."

"He was taken to a children's service," said Megan, looking at her father. "It was the day when a village child had died. He made Eliza read the service to him afterwards. He likes that sort of thing."

"He always listens at prayers," said Henry.

"And you do not?" said Cassius.

"I listen like other people. Toby is different."

"I should not have believed it. It is a most unsuitable thing. And if you call it reverent, I do not."

"I think I do," said Flavia. "Indeed, I am sure of it. I had the sense of guilt that I have in church."

"He brings back Mr. Fabian to me, sir," said William, recalling to Cassius a brother in the Church who had died in estrangement from him. "He is the living spit and will be more so."

Cassius was silent, and Bennet approached from the house, holding her hands under her apron and emitting song. She smiled easily on the children.

"Miss Bennet, what do you think of this?" said Cassius.

"A child of Toby's age conducting a funeral, and with a knowledge that had to be seen to be believed! What is your view of it? I wish to know."

"Did he?" said Bennet, looking at Toby in incredulity and admiration. "Fancy his doing a thing like that!"

"Do you think it is as it should be?"

"Oh, yes," said Bennet, gathering up Toby and regarding him with a mild concern that gave place to reassurance. "It is quite natural. It does not mean anything."

"A funeral in church seems to have made a deep impression on him."

"Oh, no," said Bennet, looking again at Toby and hitching him into an easier position on her arm. "He is not at all upset. He likes anything in the way of a ceremony. It was the same with the village play."

"It is Mr. Fabian again, sir," said William. "Preaching and play-acting go together. There is a lot in common."

Cassius again said nothing. They had gone together in the case of his brother, with whom he had quarrelled in consequence of it.

"I suppose we are going to have tea to-day," said Henry.

"Upon my word I cannot tell you," said his father. "It is time for you all to be asleep."

"It is a little late," said Bennet. "I thought it was best to get the funeral over."

"Miss Bennet, your attitude to a funeral! I feel I have never known you. I am seeing you for the first time."

"It is a mole's funeral," said Henry. "A mole is not a human being."

"It is the confusion between them that is my point."

"That is only in your own mind. It has not been in anyone else's."

"What is that writing?" said Cassius, indicating a piece of cardboard on the grave, and stepping nearer to it.

> " 'My name is Mole.
> I lie here buried deep.

45

I rest beneath this scroll
And fold my hands in everlasting sleep.'

Who wrote that?"

"I did," said Megan.

"What is its purpose?"

"It is the inscription on the grave."

"Well, why not put it there openly?"

"I did. I have just done it."

"There seemed to be something surreptitious about it."

"There wasn't anything," said Henry.

"People can't be very open about poems," said Guy, with a flush. "Anyone who is a poet knows that."

"And are you a poet?" said his father.

"Not as good a one as Megan."

"Who helped you?" said Cassius to the latter.

"No one. Guy printed the words."

"So yours was the secondary part," said Cassius to his son. "It is a strange game."

"You seemed to think it was not a game," said Henry.

"And so did all of you. You were as solemn as mutes over it. No wonder Toby was in a state of confusion."

"He was in a state of bliss," said Flavia, "the rare bliss of self-fulfilment. We will not grudge it to him. It will not come too often."

"Grudge it?" said her husband, drawing his brows together. "Who would grudge anyone anything? What a strange idea!"

"It is a very good poem for so young a child. And Guy has printed it beautifully."

"It is your own child who has done the intellectual part."

"As it happens on this occasion. It might not on another."

"Then would you draw so much attention to it?"

"It was you who did that. No one else would have done so."

"That is what I thought. It seemed to be somehow surreptitious."

"It was quite open. That is how you came to see it."

" 'My name is Mole,' " said Cassius, turning again to the grave. "I might as well say 'My name is Man'."

"The mole had no name of its own," said Henry. "It couldn't be done as it would for a person."

Cassius repeated the lines to himself.

"Again," said Toby, arrested by them.

Cassius repeated them, and Toby listened in enjoyment.

"Again."

"No, no. I can't keep on saying them."

"Again," said Toby, with ominous urgency.

Flavia repeated the lines, and the task was taken up by Bennet, as she carried Toby away. When her memory failed, Toby was able to correct her.

" 'My name is Joy,' " said Cassius, frowning to himself. "I seem to remember something of the kind, something by some poet."

"Megan was not copying anything," said Guy. "She wrote the poem out of her head."

"Ah, ha!" said his father. "So it was out of someone else's, and I daresay the better for that. I thought it was rather professional somehow; it struck me at once. And then it touched a chord of memory. I am not much of a hand at poetry, but I was equal to that. It came on me all in a flash."

"It may be an echo," said Flavia, "but it was probably unconscious. And it is a small matter."

"Well, we may as well be clear about these things. It is as well to take advantage of what we read and remember. I recognised it in a moment. I was not in a second's doubt."

"Now has no one any sense of time?" said Miss Ridley, approaching with an even tread. "And does no one hear a bell? And has no one any desire for tea?"

"I heard the bell a long time ago," said Cassius.

"Then why did you not say so?" said his wife.

"Well, why should I think everyone else was deaf?"

"I wish you were my pupil, Mr. Clare," said Miss Ridley, causing Henry and Megan to exchange a glance. "We seem to be in a class by ourselves."

"So you read poetry with them, Miss Ridley," said Cassius, certainly using a tone of fellow-feeling. "I daresay it is a good thing to do. I have read some poetry myself and remember it."

"Are you clairvoyant, Mr. Clare, that you can tell what I do by looking at me?"

Cassius betrayed that he did not judge her by this method, by motioning her towards the grave.

"Why, there is original work on foot. Now to whom do we owe this?"

"To Megan," said Henry.

"Well, well, we will not say to whom we owe it," said Cassius. "And I forget the name of the poet myself. It is the verse that I remember."

"Why, it is very nice, Megan," said Miss Ridley. "It is at once true and imaginative, and the lettering is very neat. Well, I think it is a fortunate mole to have such a funeral."

"You know it is not," said Henry.

"Guy printed it," said Megan.

"And who imagined it?" said her father, shaking his head and smiling. "Well, we won't worry about that. There is no end to the mole's good fortune."

"Mr. Clare, I should suspect you of sardonic intention, if I thought it was in character," said Miss Ridley. "Now there is the bell again, and I saw Toby being carried in some time ago. He was having some verses said to him. It seems that poetry is in the air."

"It was Megan's poetry," said Henry.

"There, you see, Megan, your work is already of use. You can go to bed to-night, knowing you have produced something that exists outside yourself. That is a great thing to feel."

"You have prevented her going to bed with different feelings," said Fabian, as he followed the governess.

"Why are people's feelings so intense when they are going to bed?" said Flavia. "You would think they would be dying down."

"You might have said more to encourage Megan in her poetic efforts," said Cassius.

"Do you mean you set me the example? What a speech to come from you!"

"Not at all. You were in a position to praise her; I was not. I knew where the poem came; you took it as original. And Megan might have had the advantage of it. Children are sensitive about such things."

"You have forestalled what you deserve, but that shows you know you deserve it."

"Shall we leave this thing?" said her husband, with a gesture towards the inscription. "Or would it be fairer to everyone to get rid of it?"

"What do you think yourself?"

Cassius glanced at it again, and as if thinking better of taking any trouble, lifted his shoulders and turned away. He gained on the children and Miss Ridley and walked behind them.

"Is Father happy?" said Guy.

"He is often satisfied," said Megan. "You can see him having the satisfaction."

"There is a great deal about grown-up people that children cannot understand," said Miss Ridley.

"And a great deal that they can," said Fabian. "That is where the danger lies."

"I don't think there is much to understand about Father," said Megan. "When he is unhappy himself, he wants other people to be."

"You cannot judge human beings as simply as that," said Miss Ridley. "They are complex creatures with many conflicting qualities."

"Ah, your father never wants you to be unhappy, my

49

little one," said Cassius, quickening his pace. "It is true that he is sometimes unhappy and uncertain, but he never wants to hurt his children. And it was a beautiful poem; it has made him proud of you. And if it shows you read poetry yourself, he is even prouder. But he has his own troubles. You must not expect him always to hide it. Miss Ridley is right that we have different qualities."

"I think there is generally one chief one," said Megan.

"Well, tell us the chief ones of the people you know." said Miss Ridley, in an easy tone.

"Yours is wanting to learn all you can, as long as you do what is right. Bennet's is kindness; I think that is the best. Mater's is fairness to everyone and a sort of cleverness in herself. Fabian's is anger because he hasn't his real mother. I don't think Guy has his yet. Toby's is wanting the best of things for himself, and I think it always will be."

"And what is Megan's?" said Cassius. "A power of insight into the human heart?"

"There was a lot that was true in what she said," said Henry. "And none of them is really a happy quality."

"Oh, dear, oh, dear!" said his father.

"Yes," said Henry, meeting his eyes. "That is what ought to be said. But people don't like you to say it."

"If they did, they would get a good deal of pleasure from you. As it is, they get something else. There is not so much difference between you and me, if what you think of me is true."

"You should not have heard what we said."

"Of course I should. It was my duty to hear it. A father has to know his children, in order to make his plans for them. I shall have to think of mine for you."

"You are threatening to take revenge."

"Revenge? On whom and for what?" said Cassius, throwing up his brows. "Oh, you are the object for it, are you?"

"Now come indoors," said Miss Ridley. "You are too

fond of the sound of your own voices. It seems that this afternoon will never end."

When Henry and Megan entered the nursery, their faces cleared at the sight that met them. Bennet and Eliza were seated at the table, and Toby, in his chair and reconciled to the position, was murmuring in a satisfied way to himself.

"Ashes and ashes. Dust and dust. Poor little mole have dear little hands! Smaller than Toby's; very small hands. Poor mole buried very deep. But very nice box and wake up again to-morrow. William come to church; yes, poor William! Bennet give Toby some first. Not Megan; Toby!"

His voice rose to a shriek and Bennet supplied him at once, an order of precedence that his brother and sister did not question.

CHAPTER IV

A<small>INGER STRODE ACROSS</small> the kitchen and pulled his chair from the table.

"Well, we have reached a parting of the ways. There is to be a crossing of our threshold."

"In what shape?" said the upper housemaid.

"Ah, Kate, that is asking a question."

"So it is," said Mrs. Frost, the cook.

"And do you expect me to answer it?" said Ainger, leaning back.

"Yes," said Mrs. Frost.

"Well, I will not disappoint you. I will specify the shape, as Kate expresses it. It is to be that of the former mistress."

"So she is to be allowed access?" said Kate.

"That is the word," said Ainger, in sympathy with it.

"And what a word!" said the general man, finding himself less so. "So this is what education does for you."

"It might have done more for us," said Kate's assistant. "We might be in houses of our own."

"The damp and cramp would be your own too," said Halliday. "They wouldn't be anyone else's. Look at Mrs. Frost, presiding at her table as if she were under her own roof."

"Must you look at me?" said the latter, with her eyes down.

Mrs. Frost was a short woman of fifty-eight, with a figure that expanded from shoulders to hips, a flat-featured, ruddy face, and large, shallow-set, hazel eyes, that seemed to fall before they revealed their expression. Thomas Halliday was a lean, wiry man over sixty, with a long, scraggy neck, cheeks at once leathery and pendulous, indignant, greenish eyes and a habit of throwing back his head in token of disgust. He had been in the household for nearly fifty years, and had advanced from page-boy to general man and advanced no further. There was something about him that disqualified him for personal attendance on the family. Mrs. Frost had been asked if she knew what it was, and had replied simply that she did.

"Your place was given you out of esteem for your parents," he said to the under-housemaid. "You were fortunate to get it."

"But was it a mark of esteem for me?" said Madge.

"Esteem may come," said Ainger. "Personally I have no complaint."

"And the family did not know you apart from any other lad."

"They did not, Halliday. But they know me now. I think they would say so." Ainger leant back in his chair and threw one leg over the other in the manner of his master.

"I am content to be what I am," said Halliday. "Would not you say the same, Mrs. Frost?"

"No," said the latter.

"And a contented mind is a continual feast."

"And the only feast you will get," said Madge. "So it is as well to be satisfied with it."

"A continual feast," murmured Mrs. Frost, glancing at the stove behind her. "I should have a contented mind."

"What more do I want?" said Halliday.

"You don't want anything more," said Madge. "That may be why you don't have it."

"What better work is there than ours? What kind is more respectable or accorded more respect?"

"Most kinds," said Mrs. Frost.

"What kind accords more respect to other people?" said Madge.

"I do not grudge it," said Ainger. "If you think I do, you mistake my attitude."

Madge gave a laugh that seemed to be meant to be

heard, and turned her eyes about her. Her large, blue eyes and full-coloured face seemed more insistent than herself, and she was more aware of them. Her figure was short and ungainly, but of this she did not allow herself to be aware. Her superior had a tall, trim form, small, inconsistent features, small, round, dark eyes and an air of general acceptance of things. Madge was thirty and Kate forty-six, and both looked about their age. They were companions rather than friends, and would have parted without distress.

"Well, has the master one wife or two?" said Madge. "It seems that the higher you are, the more you can have. Solomon had hundreds."

"And was said to be the wisest man," said Kate, in a serious tone. "But I doubt if the master is wise in transcending the number."

"The higher you are, the more you can have of a good many things," said Ainger.

"Always wanting more, more, more!" said Halliday.

"I cannot imagine you a wife, Mrs. Frost," said Kate.

"Neither can I."

"Haven't you ever been one?"

"You can see what I have been."

"Are you ashamed of not being one?" said Madge, laughing.

"Yes," said Mrs. Frost.

"Mr. Halliday ought to propose to you."

"Are you sure he has not done so, Mrs. Frost?" said Ainger. "Your secret would be safe with me."

A boy of fourteen entered the room, came to his seat and began at once to eat, as though to cover some consciousness.

"Well, Simon," said Halliday, without expression.

"Well, my lad," said Ainger, with one of authority and threat.

"He has put on his page's suit," said Madge, in a tone of mild excitement.

"How long is it since you discarded it, Mr. Ainger?" said Kate. "The very same suit, if I remember."

"You do remember," said Mrs. Frost.

"Twenty-four years," said Ainger. "Ten years before the boy was born."

"So the world was prepared for his entry," said Kate, sighing.

"He has polished the buttons!" said Madge.

"The only improvement he could make," said Ainger. "And I never thought it was one. It drew attention to the garb."

"It is comical," said Kate, in acquiescence. "But it suits Simon better than it did you. He looks more at home in it."

"That is what he is. He is born and bred for what it indicates."

"And what were you born and bred for?" said Halliday.

"I was bred for that, Halliday. I make no secret of it. I was born for something else, and I can feel I have attained it."

"Put into words what you have attained."

"Ah, it is difficult to do that for you, Halliday," said Ainger, leaning back with an appraising eye on his colleague.

"Simon left school yesterday," said Madge.

"It is not very difficult to leave something off," said Kate.

"Did he find that knowledge was power?" said Mrs. Frost.

"Money is power," said Simon. "And you get money by working."

"Not much for your kind of work," said Ainger.

"It is the same kind as yours."

"Now remember this," said Ainger, leaning towards him. "You know nothing about my kind of work, and will always know nothing. It is hidden from your eyes."

"And from a good many people's," said Halliday.

"When Mr. Ainger rises further," said Madge, "we

shall remember that we sat at the same table with him in his humble days."

"And he will remember your doing so, Madge," said Ainger.

"Will he return to claim one of us?" said Mrs. Frost.

Madge looked towards the window with wide eyes.

"Whomever I married," said Kate, "I should not forget my early associates."

"You would be too weighed down and worried to remember anything," said Halliday. "You are better as you are."

"Talking of marriages," said Kate, "the master's situation invites enquiry."

"I can meet it," said Ainger. "I have his confidence. He feels that a mother's feelings command respect. I am a confidential servant."

"For what that is worth," said Halliday.

"It is worth something to the rest of us," said Madge, "as we are the other kind."

"Everyone is a servant in his way," said Halliday. "There is no essential difference."

"Only an actual one," said Mrs. Frost.

"It is hard to see how anyone in Mr. Ainger's situation can rise higher," said Kate. "If there was any method, we might all resort to it."

A bell sounded in the passage and Simon became alert.

"Answer it, my boy," said Halliday. "Your moment has come."

"Yes, answer it," said Ainger. "I don't want to insist on the prerogative."

Simon did so and returned flushed and satisfied.

"I did what they wanted. They said they hoped I would do well."

"Well, it is to their advantage," said Kate. "But they confront their own demands."

"And fulfil them," said Ainger. "You see it when you are in contact."

"Will the two Mrs. Clares become acquainted?" said Kate. "That is the question I have been asking myself."

"And what answer did you give yourself?" said Ainger.

"It seems there is bound to be encounter."

"What is it to do with us?" said Halliday.

"As much as anyone's affairs are to do with anyone else," said Ainger. "That is, nearly as much to do with us as our own."

"And a cat may look at a king," said Kate, with a sigh.

"I do not see myself in that light," said Halliday, "and I have reason to think other people do not. Talking of being a cat, Ainger, we might as well say a laughing hyaena."

Ainger leant back and did his best to establish the comparison, and Halliday opened his mouth and did no more. The bell rang again and was answered by Simon, who returned and crossed the kitchen with a withdrawn expression.

"The ash-trays forgotten," said Ainger, idly.

"By whom?" said Halliday.

"By me. I have other things to think of."

"The master's affairs," said Kate. "It is true we are dependent on you for them."

"Yes, he and I often indulge in a masculine talk. I am asked for my opinion. But I sometimes know better than to give it." Ainger shook his head.

"Are you not allowed to disagree?" said Madge.

"It tends to be complex, Madge. As must arise from contact."

"The trays were not polished," said Simon, as he returned.

"They will be in future," said Ainger. "And by you. Say 'Yes, sir'."

"Yes, sir," said Simon, without reluctance.

"He promises," said Kate, resting her eyes on Simon.

"If I were the mistress," said Madge, "I would not consent to meet the first Mrs. Clare."

57

"You would do what your place required of you," said Ainger. "You betray your unfitness."

"Well, fitness for it would not be much good to me."

"It would not help her," said Kate.

"I can imagine Mrs. Frost in any place," said Halliday.

"So can I," said Mrs. Frost. "I have done so."

"Not that we should like your present place to be filled by anyone else."

"A sentiment I endorse," said Ainger.

"I hardly expected this," said Mrs. Frost, looking down. Simon laughed, and Ainger looked at him sternly.

"The boy may listen to the talk," said Kate.

"But not suggest commentary on it."

The bell rang once more, and Simon returned from answering it and addressed Ainger.

"You are to answer the bell yourself, and not always send me."

"Not always send you!" said Ainger, rising and leaning towards him. "Answer the bell myself! Answer it myself, did you say? Tell me what they really said."

"They said what I told you. It is not my fault."

"Answer the bell myself!" said Ainger, his feet moving rapidly. "That is what you say to me! Say it again, and let me see what they meant by it."

"I see," said Mrs. Frost.

"So do I," said Halliday.

The bell rang again with some force, and Ainger sped from the room as if he also saw it.

"A confidential servant seems much the same as any other," said Halliday.

"They may want to make some confidence," said Madge.

"I suppose they always do," said Mrs. Frost.

"There is nothing incompatible," said Kate.

"Serving other people can't take us so far," said Halliday.

"It must take them further," said Kate. "It is to be accepted."

Ainger returned with a flushed face, humming to himself, and sat down idly in his place.

"Fetch me that parcel on the pantry table," he said to Simon presently.

Simon brought it to him.

"Unpack it," said Ainger sharply, as if the direction should have been superfluous.

Simon disclosed a box of cigars, and Ainger took it and strolled to the door.

"So the cigars spend a time with Mr. Ainger before they go to the master," said Madge.

"There is no need to form pictures," said Kate.

Ainger returned with some cigars in his hand, sat down and felt for matches.

"A mark of the master's regard," he said as he lighted one. "I thought it was wise to answer the bell."

"So did I," said Mrs. Frost.

"Ah, people can't always take your place," said Halliday, with his eyes on the cigars.

Ainger handed him one, as if in response to a request, and he began to smoke.

"You haven't reached this stage yet, Simon."

"No, and I never shall. It is a waste of money."

"Not when you don't pay for the cigars," said Madge.

"Well, that is on some occasions," said Ainger, "when the master feels in a comradely mood."

"The parcel was addressed to the master. Why wasn't it taken to him?"

"Was he to unpack it himself?"

"It wasn't sugar or tea."

"And if it had been, you might have had designs on it yourself," said Ainger, producing mirth and ignoring it.

"In all the years I have been in this house," said Halliday, "I have never had a cigar offered me."

"Neither have I," said Mrs. Frost.

"Well, it happens to me sometimes," said Ainger, watching the smoke rise from his.

"I wonder the master likes to ring for you," said Madge.

"I don't know that he does. I sometimes catch a hint that it goes a little against the grain. He is in the grip of circumstances."

"He has a peremptory hand on the bell," said Kate. "Not that it is an indication."

"It is generally the mistress who rings. And with regard to her I have no claim."

"I have a respect for the mistress."

"And she would expect it, Kate, and is entitled. But my bond is with the master. And it would not be with both. There are reasons."

"And they not on good terms?" said Madge.

"It is complex, Madge; a term I have used before."

"Will someone fetch me some apples from the storehouse?" said Mrs. Frost.

Ainger gave a nod to Simon, and he rose and left the room. In the hall he encountered the sons of the house on their way to the garden.

"Well, Simon," said Fabian.

"Good afternoon, sir," said Simon.

"Can you have a game with us?" said Guy.

"I have left school, sir," said Simon, with a note of surprise.

"Very nice boy," said Toby, whose hand was held by Fabian.

"What do you want to be when you grow up?" said Henry.

"Very nice buttons," added Toby.

"A butler, sir," said Simon.

"Would you rather be a butler than a king?" said Henry, struck by something in the tone.

"Well, perhaps not, sir," said Simon, brought to face with another kind of advancement.

As the talk went on, Toby disengaged his hand and wandered about the hall. He saw a vase on the table and sent his eyes from it to his brothers. Then he went behind the table and threw it on the ground, and as it broke, gave himself to guarded mirth, hampered by further glances. Then he rejoined the group and placed his hand in Fabian's.

Bennet came singing down the stairs.

"Why, look at that vase! Has any one of you touched it?"

"We did not know it was there," said Fabian.

Toby kept his eyes on Simon.

"Oh, dear, oh, dear!" said Henry, looking after the latter. "I don't want to be a servant. And if I did, I could be one and be happy."

"Fabian hold Toby's hand too tight," said Toby, frowning and pulling it away.

"It kept you out of mischief," said his brother.

"Very good boy," said Toby.

CHAPTER V

"Ursula, our hour has come," said Elton Scrope. "I mean, of course, that the hour has come. The occasion is upon us."

"And we do not deserve an occasion. No one deserves anything so good or so bad. We all deserve so little."

"A sister is returning to us, who was said to be our second mother, and who must have been that, as what is said is always true; a sister who wrote weekly letters and watched over us from afar."

"And now will watch over us in our own home. No, we do not deserve it."

"We have had such a dear, little, narrow life. Will Catherine broaden and enrich it? I could not bear a wealth of experience. It will be enough to live with someone who has had it."

"She will be too occupied with adding to it to want to share it," said Ursula.

"So we do want the occasion. My heart told me we did. We are jealous of her other life. It is a natural, ordinary emotion, but I do think we can claim it."

"What is the good of a second mother, if she becomes the first mother of other people? No one likes the second place. No place at all is different. We will not say if we should like that."

"Will you give up the housekeeping?"

"Yes. I resent being supplanted, but I am glad to give it up. I don't mind the trivial task, but I dislike being known to do it. I am sensitive to opinion."

"Most people are that."

"I don't think they can be, when I am."

"Don't you take any interest in household things? I take so much."

"I want to have a soul above them, and to be thought to have one."

"I have a soul just on their level. Do you think we have souls?"

"No," said Ursula.

"Do you mind that?"

"Not yet; I am only thirty-two; but when I am older I shall mind it; when extinction is imminent. Now it is too far away."

"We may die at any moment."

"Not you and I. It is other people who may die young."

"Why should we be exceptions?"

"I don't know. I wonder what the reasons are?"

"You don't think you and I will have an eternity together?"

"No, but we shall have until we are seventy. And there is no difference."

"Can you bear not to have the real thing?"

"No," said his sister.

"Then when you are older, will you begin to have beliefs?"

"No, I shall realise the hopelessness of things. I shall meet it face to face."

"And will you be proud of doing that?"

"Well, think how few people can do it. And I must have some compensation; it will not be much."

"I shall not be able to face it. I shall begin to say we cannot be quite sure."

"And I shall like to hear you say it. Even a spurious comfort is better than nothing."

"Is it unusual to dread the return of someone to whom we owe so much?"

"We do dread people to whom we owe things. The debt ought to be paid, and anyone dreads that. But our debt to Catherine is of the sort we cannot repay."

"That is the most difficult kind," said Elton.

"That is the conventional view. And convention is usually so sound that it is right to be a slave to it. But it is not in this case."

"Then we should look forward to her coming."

"I am getting quite excited," said his sister.

"Not as excited as I am. I must rise and pace the room."

"And I will keep my seat by an effort."

Ursula Scrope had a tall, thin figure, narrow, dark, spectacled eyes, features of regular type, but displaying sundry twists and turns, long, useless-looking hands, and limbs so loosely hung that they seemed to be insecurely joined to her body. Her brother was two years younger and of similar type, with a rounder, fuller face, rounder, lighter eyes, and the peculiarities of feature modified. It was clear that their relation went deep and would last for their lives.

"Ought we to count the minutes to the arrival?" he said. "I believe we should have had a calendar and crossed out the days."

"How does one get a calendar?"

"I think they are sent at Christmas, though I don't know why. I suppose Catherine will know."

"So she will. How restful it will be! We shall cease to think for ourselves. We ought never to have done so. What was the good of a second mother?"

"We shall relapse into childhood," said Elton. "No one ever really comes out of it. That is why life is such a strain. We have to pretend."

"And why people's stories of their childhood are always their best. They don't really know about anything else. To write about it, they would have to be original. And they cannot be that."

"Will Catherine be proud of us?"

"No. Why should she be?"

"Ursula, don't you see any reasons?"

64

"Yes, but she will not see them. Her children will take all her pride."

"And yet you are excited by her coming?"

"Well, it will take away that strange nostalgia for something that has no name."

"Will it? I thought I had just to carry it with me."

"The arrival!" said Ursula, looking out of the window. "What a good thing the luggage takes the whole of the trap! It is dreadful to meet people at the station. They see you as you really are. It is a thing that does not happen anywhere else."

"I thought it happened chiefly in our own homes."

"People learn to ignore things there. And at a station they simply confront them."

"Well, my brother and sister!" said a quick, deep voice, as a small, dark woman came rapidly into the room, talking in short, quick sentences. "My desertion of you is over. Have you minded it as much as I have? If so, you are as glad as I am. But the culprit is the one who suffers. It is one of the fair things in life. And I shall alter it all for you. I shall tell you its meaning. And you will see it as I do."

"I always fail at moments of test," said Ursula, as she bent towards her sister. "I cannot carry things off."

"You are yourself. As I looked to find you. I would not have you rise to an occasion. I should feel you were someone else."

"But a more manageable person."

"Not the person I looked to see. Not my sister."

"Do you think I am a success?" said Elton. "I have meant my silence to cover so much."

"You are both yourselves. You have stood the years. My anxiety was in myself. I felt that change had come to me. I feared it might threaten you. But the onslaught of life has been easier on you. May it always be."

"But we do not seem people who have not lived?" said her brother.

"You have not lived much yet. Your time is to come."

"Mine is not," said Ursula. "I tolerate nothing that looms ahead. I will not be threatened by life."

"I am rather flattered by that," said Elton. "I should have thought it would pass me by."

"There is no threat yet," said Catherine. "Your sky is clear. May it never darken. And now we leave the heights and depths. I see we are rescued from them. Ursula will deal with the tea to-day. I will be the guest. Anything she has done for years, she can do once more."

Ursula made some adjustment on the tray and yielded her place to her brother.

"Does Elton pour out the tea?"

"Yes," said the latter, with his eyes on doing so. "My touch is as sensitive as any woman's."

"More sensitive than Ursula's?"

"No, but more successful."

"This is a thing I had not imagined. I suppose there will be others."

"No," said Ursula. "I think this is the only one."

Catherine looked from her brother to her sister.

"You have had your feeling for each other. I did not take that. What if you had not had it? What should I have done?"

"Would you not have done what you have now?" said Ursula.

"I should. It is the truth. I will not fear it. But how we should have suffered, both of you and I!"

"Are you going to see Cassius?" said Elton. "The question does not savour of curiosity."

"It simply contains it," said Catherine, smiling. "I shall see my sons. I shall know them. They will know me. I may or may not see their father. That means nothing."

"You have taken a brave step. Fancy my being able to say a thing like that! I don't think Ursula's lips could have framed the words."

66

"It was easy to take the step. I had to do so, knowing I was breaking faith. That had been a thing I could not do. I found I could do nothing else."

"I wonder if I could face reality," said Elton.

"What do you call this?" said Catherine, taking his hand and laying it on Ursula's. "The feeling between you. What is that?"

"The foundation of our life. All lives must have a foundation. I was thinking of the things that come after it."

"It is best to have a foundation and not to build on it," said Ursula.

"Foundations! Mine were torn from under me. I allowed it myself. I confused the incident with the essence. I have paid the price."

Catherine Clare had a short, spare figure, straight, rather handsome features, iron-grey, curling hair and dark eyes that seemed to realise their own swift glance. Her voice was a quick, deep monotone, and all her movements were directed to what she did.

"You are an accomplished tea-maker, Elton. I shall hesitate to take your place."

"I have always hesitated," said Ursula. "I am uncertain of myself. It is a thing that is known about me, I think the only one."

"You are proud of it," said Catherine, smiling.

"Well, I hope people think I am. They don't despise you for things, if you are proud of them. They don't seem to mind a low standard."

"It is important to rinse every cup with hot water," said Elton, doing as he said.

"You will find my casual methods a change," said Catherine. "I hope you will not mind them."

"Ursula will not. I shall mind them very much. But wild horses would not drag it from me. Though I hardly think wild horses do as much to drag things from people as is thought."

Catherine gave her quick, deep laugh.

"I could never give anything more attention than I felt it deserved," she said.

"But food deserves all attention. And tea is an English-woman's favourite meal. And her standard is mine."

"And is it also Ursula's?"

"I strive to make it so," said the latter, "and I am proud if I succeed. I am a person with my own pathos. But I hope no one knows that."

"I wonder if I am," said Elton. "Or is my pathos so much my own that it does not count?"

"What does it consist of?" said Catherine.

"Of asking so little of life. Of feeling that is all I deserve. Of being afraid to publish what I write, for fear people should read it. Of being glad that I cannot afford to marry, in case I should do so."

"You would not have to marry because you could afford to."

"People do seem to have to," said Elton.

"Would you like to marry, Ursula?"

"No, but I wish people believed it. I don't like to have any pathos but my own."

"Why do you not want to?"

"I could not give a house those unmistakable signs of a woman's presence. I do not even recognise them."

"I hardly think I gave my house those signs."

"Then perhaps Cassius had his own pathos. And I see it must have been his own. I don't wonder you could not bear it."

"There were things I could not bear," said Catherine, in a just audible tone.

"I could not bear anything. I shut my eyes to that side of life."

"What do you know about life?" said her sister.

"Everyone knows all about it. It is impossible to help it, though it is best not to put it into words."

"Tell me what you know."

"Let me do it," said Elton. "It is not short and will not

soon be gone. It is longer than anyone can realise. And it is very brave to end it. To say it is cowardly is absurd. It is only said by people who would not dare to do it."

"Some people dare to face life," said Catherine.

"Most people do," said Ursula. "We are talking of facing death."

"I never feel disapproval," said Elton. "It is a feeling foreign to my nature. I hardly need to know all to forgive all. Considering the pleasure of knowing, that is only fair. I can hardly bear to know it; I forgive so much. I think people do such understandable things."

"Yes," said Ursula; "I am often ashamed of understanding them."

"I hope I understood," said Catherine, looking straight before her. "I hope I had sympathy. I hope I did not give it only to myself. I wonder if I knew my husband's nature. I wonder if I recognised its signs."

"Signs are not things we can be expected to study," said her brother.

"I wonder if I measured our difference. I was of another character. I did not look for thrust or insult. I never retaliated, but I forget none. The load of memory became too great. He did not know what I carried with me. His burden was light."

"We sometimes see the boys in the distance. They are growing up."

"Yes, I have missed their childhood. I have faced it every day, given each its own loss."   .

"I have said an insensitive thing, and I did not think I could. It is terrible to know oneself. I hope I shall never get to know the whole."

"Do they know I am here?" said Catherine.

"Yes, they must know. Our servants talk to theirs. I listen to servants' gossip. It is one of my weaknesses and my pleasures."

"They are often the same," said Ursula. "Perhaps they always are."

"No wonder we do not conquer our failings," said Catherine.

"Do you wish you had stayed with your husband?" said her brother.

"I found I could not stay. I took the way that offered. I accepted the gain and loss. Or I thought I did. But I find I cannot do so. I am breaking my word. I have lost so much, that I have lost myself."

"How do you feel about the boys living with their father?" said Ursula.

"I would take nothing from them. I have learned to measure loss. And in a way it means nothing. He is a dead figure in my heart. I could meet him and say my word. I could see him go, the same dead thing. But to his children he is alive."

"I wonder what he means to them."

"I have wondered it night and day."

"I do enjoy this personal talk," said Elton. "I know I ought to be ashamed, but creditable pleasure is so hard."

"Like rejoicing in other's joy," said Ursula. "Though that is an extreme case."

"They do say we should eschew the personal and pursue wider things," said Catherine.

"It would serve them right to have to do it," said her sister. "If they had to fulfil their boasts, what a lesson it would be! They ought to be made to talk about national affairs."

"Well, people do talk about such things."

"So I have heard," said Elton, "but I do not want any proof."

"If you listen to servants, you must find the men sometimes talk of them," said Catherine.

"I listen to the women. It is some instinct of self-protection. And it is their standard I admire, their integrity of interest and purity of aim. What a good thing there are so many more of them than men!"

"The men tend to be more reliable witnesses."

"Yes, and they are not ashamed of it. Not ashamed of being without creative power. No woman would be so shameless. She would have no friends. No other woman would tolerate it."

"She might have men friends."

"Well, that would be her punishment."

"I suppose some men talk of personal things."

"There are some happy marriages," said Ursula. "So they must."

"A man is supposed to eat his breakfast with the paper propped up before him," said Catherine.

"Well, he has to quote from it and pretend he thought it all himself," said Elton. "But I don't suppose Cassius did that."

"No, he tended to the personal. But the personal note must be the real one. It ends the interest of things, if they are not rooted in the truth."

"Sometimes it adds to it," said Ursula. "That seems to be its purpose. How it does add to it! It even does for the whole."

"Distortion seems always to tend to people's disadvantage."

"Well, it may as well kill two birds with one stone."

"What good does it do us to disparage people?"

"I am not sure, but it seems to be great good. Perhaps it makes us better by comparison."

"Do we do everything for our own advantage?"

"Yes, I think we do. No one else does anything for it. So it takes all our time to get enough done."

"I have a dislike of the simple sin of saying behind people's backs what we do not say to their faces," said Catherine, with a little laugh.

"It does seem strange of you to have anything to do with what is simple."

"It would be a more complex sin to do both," said Elton.

"It would be better than only doing the first," said Catherine.

"I thought the first was always done," said her sister.

"I suppose criticism may be honest. Or is that the most unkindest cut of all."

"Well, it is always a cut," said Ursula.

"Is it necessary to indulge in any kind of disparagement?"

"Well, it is a temptation," said Elton. "Look at your word, 'indulge'. And we are only told to make an exception of the dead."

"And it is no good to say behind people's backs what can never get round to them," said Ursula.

A servant opened the door and spoke to Catherine.

"Will you see Mr. Clare, ma'am? And if so, would you prefer to see him alone?"

"I will see him," said Catherine, after a moment's pause. "And it need not be alone. He can come in here."

"This is more than I hoped for," said Elton to Ursula. "Is it almost too much? Can we bear it?"

"How can I tell? It will be a scene from life, and I have never met one."

"I think I can face it," said her brother, placing himself where he could do so.

Cassius entered the room with his usual deliberate stride, keeping his eyes from anyone's face.

"Well, Catherine, I thought it was best to take the bull by the horns. Preparing for the interview and working ourselves up would do no good. So I braced myself up and acted on the spur of the moment. And standing in front of you as I am, I still think it was the right thing. I often find my impulses lead me in the right direction. This isn't by any means the first case of it. Well, how are you, Catherine, after all these years? It is best to ask the question in the usual way. The less awkwardness, the better. You are very little changed."

"Perhaps to your eyes. To me the change is great."

"Well, no one would know it. I don't know how much I

72

am changed myself. I expect you would have recognised me."

"There is little outward difference."

"Well, as I say, I took my courage in my hands and came before I had time to think. A deadlock would not have served us. Well, it is a long time since we met."

"Yes, it is nine years."

"Not since Fabian was a child of four."

"Not since then."

"You would be surprised to see him now."

"As a boy of thirteen? No, that is how I think of him."

"So we are to let the dead past bury its dead?"

"The past is dead," said Catherine, in a low tone. "It has no dead to bury. My sons' lives are young."

"Yes, that is true. But they have had a good mother in my wife."

"They have had a good woman with them."

"You left them of your own will."

"You made it a condition. I had no choice but to leave them."

"Well, well, we need not go into that. We are to meet now on other terms. We understand each other."

"I wonder if you understand me. I have not helped you. I have returned to my own place. That place is near my children. I will not go further. I will not say it is with them. I have come back to see them, to know them, to break my faith. I have not the power to keep it. For years it has been growing too much for me. It has grown too much. I would rather see them with your sanction. I would not impose on them further burdens. I do not know how much they have borne."

"They have nothing to bear, and will have nothing. But I understand your wish to see them. We can probably arrange a meeting. It is a simple thing."

"Is your wife willing for us to have it?"

"Well, it is a hard thing for her, Catherine. You must see that. But she is a woman who sees what is right and does it. That is the key to her nature. And it seemed to me that this was a right thing. I do not believe in being bound by the past. So I put it to her; perhaps I imposed it on her. I may do that sometimes; I daresay you remember. After all it is for me to take the lead. And she let herself be guided by me. She saw that change was gathering. Change seems to come of itself when the time is ripe. I don't think we have much to do with it. We are in the hands of unseen forces. Well, when do you want to see the boys?"

"As soon as I can. And in their home. So that I know the truth about them."

"You can come on them at any moment, and the truth will be before your eyes. If there was anything wrong, it would be a good deal by now."

"Yes, each day has done its work. It has taken them a step further."

"Ah, you have your own way of putting things, Catherine. You always had. I don't know that I mean so much less, though I sound so different. It brings things back to me: I admit that it does. How the stages of our life pass! Well, I will speak to my wife. I don't know how much it will be asking of her."

"It should not be too much. It will serve the children. She has wished to serve them."

"It has gone beyond the wish. She has given them of her best. You and I should both be grateful."

"I know it. I hardly can be. I must feel she has had what is mine."

"Well, in a way you will have what is hers. You are bound to undo her work in a measure. You will do it as little as you can. I must trust you there, Catherine, odd word though it is to pass between you and me."

"You may trust me. And I will trust her. She and I should be able to work together. It is for a common end."

"Well, you are both so unusual that I daresay you will. Though it could not be said of any other two women. It

74

has been my lot to be cast with a strange pair. It is not for me to give advice, especially as neither of you ever takes it. I declare I begin to couple you together in my mind. Well, good-bye, Catherine. I suppose we shall meet sometimes in this new way. And we bear each other no grudge. I will do my best, if you will do yours. Good-bye."

There was silence after he had gone.

"Do you really bear him no grudge?" said Ursula.

"I have no feeling about him. If I had, it could only be of its kind. I make no claim to his sort of generosity."

"So you do bear him one," said Elton. "It throws light on the scene. That came from the depths of human experience, and I faced it to the end. I cannot be what I thought."

"I kept my eyes away from it," said Ursula. "I did not hear more than I could help. Cassius is the man he always was."

"He is not a man to me," said Catherine.

"You are still a woman to him," said her brother.

"Elton, do not talk like everyone else," said Ursula. "Even Cassius does not do that."

"I will try not to. But I almost wish I were like them. I think I will be. Catherine, you wanted to marry Cassius. Did you really wish it from your heart?"

"I wanted to marry. Many women do. I wanted to have children. Many women want that too. And why should they not want it? And Cassius offered it to me. Does it need to be so much explained? I am like everyone else. There is the matter in a word."

"I wonder what is bringing out the worst in me," said Elton. "It is hard not to do oneself justice at such a time; one of those times that will stand out in people's memories. I dread the moment when this stands out in yours. And I am talking about myself, when my every thought should be of you. And Ursula is putting me to shame by one of those silences that say more than words."

"It is such a good way of saying it," said the latter.

"Words do not come to our sister at these times," said Catherine.

"No, she appears to such advantage."

"I have hardly realised how I have missed you, Elton. Missed you both."

"I am used to being an afterthought," said Ursula. "I think it brings out my especial quality. There is a peculiar grace in taking the second place, and I think I may have a grace, if it is peculiar."

"You both have your own place with me, as you always had."

"Catherine comes out of herself to say comfortable words to us," said Elton. "And in her situation! And we in ours, that is hardly one at all, are remaining in ourselves as if it were the proper place to be."

"When no one should ever be there really," said Ursula.

"You are both there less than most people," said Catherine.

"Perhaps we should live in other people's lives, if we saw them," said her brother. "I found myself living in Cassius's life to-day. It really did seem like self-forgetfulness."

"I think that is more than can be expected of us."

"I wonder if there is such a thing," said Ursula. "It is hard to see how there can be. We think other people forget themselves because they pretend to, and we assume they think it of us in the same way. There is one thing to be said for not surviving after death. We shall not know them when they know our hearts, and when we know theirs. The second would be the worst."

"I think I always know them," said Elton. "But I do not mind. I find it so surprising that no one is all bad. It seems that we can depend on it. It seems almost too much."

"I used to feel I knew Cassius's heart," said Catherine. "And he did reveal more of it than most of us. He did not seem to know when he betrayed himself."

"Well, that would explain his doing it," said Ursula.

"Perhaps that is the difference between a bad person and a good; that the one reveals himself, and the other has the proper feeling to hide it."

"I shall see my sons," said Catherine, standing with clasped hands. "Cassius does a thing when it is before him. He is disturbed until it is done."

"I did not know he was so like me," said Ursula.

"You may see him come out in the boys," said Elton. "You should be prepared."

"I do not mind what I see. I only ask to see it. I can bear anything but the one thing."

"Would you have agreed to the conditions if you had known what they would mean?"

"I saw nothing but the moment. Just as now I see only that."

"How fulfilled I do feel!" said Elton. "All my curiosity satisfied. Even my questions answered. I don't think it has ever happened to me before. I did not know it could happen."

"I don't think it can," said Ursula. "It is one of those things like Shakespeare, that could never come again."

"The force of things carried us on," said her sister. "The truth came to the light of itself. Reticence lost its place."

"And it generally has so much, indeed almost all there is."

"There is still a question to ask," said Elton, "now we feel that nothing will be denied. Cassius still has some feeling for Catherine. Does he know it is unrequited? If he does not, it spoils it all."

"He will never know," said Catherine. "In a way he will always know nothing. And now you know enough. I ought not to have made this demand. I should have kept my life and myself in their own place."

"I cannot bear people who try to be brave," said Ursula. "There is the danger that they may succeed, and it is even worse than other kinds of success."

"Courage may certainly resemble indifference."

"It might almost be the same," said Elton. "But it is too commonplace to think it is. Does Cassius's wife know of his coming here? I am glad I am in time to ask that."

"I do not know. I would tell you, if I did."

"How can we find out?"

"I do not know. I am an unrewarding companion. I do not pretend to come out of myself."

"Well, I daresay that is always pretence," said her sister.

"I will leave you now. I will rest and let you do so. We shall spend the evening together. Our old and our new life will begin."

"Will two lives be too much for us?" said Elton, as the door closed. "When we can hardly manage one. There is something I must say to you, Ursula. I am haunted by the thought of Cassius. Beneath that exterior does there beat a faithful heart?"

"Why are such things always said to happen beneath an exterior? What other place is there for them?"

"I think they would be less heart-rending anywhere else. And that is not the only thing. I believe the iron has entered into Catherine's soul. I have wanted to meet an instance of that but I see it was a dreadful wish. I might weep, if I did not see that your feelings were too deep for tears. I must not be shallow by comparison."

CHAPTER VI

"WELL, YOU WILL not guess where I have been," said Cassius, striding across his drawing-room.

"We will not, my boy," said his father. "We will hear you tell us."

Cassius paused in his advance as space failed, and seemed at a loss for further cover.

"I will guess," said Flavia. "You have been to see your first wife."

"Yes, well, I thought I had better put my pride in my pocket," said Cassius, putting back his head and feeling in his pocket, as if it were the natural place for anything tangible or otherwise. "It was a thing to get behind me. So I set my teeth and got it behind. And it went against the grain, I can tell you. I had never imagined myself in such a place. I had to brace myself up, as if I were going to face some great ordeal. And that is what it was. It seemed to be a test of every human quality. I declare I found there were things in me I had never suspected. I seemed to have to deal with a new self."

"It brought out your better side. That is always a difficult thing to look back on."

"Yes, make a mock of it. I might have known you would. You are not a stranger to me. But it was not an easy thing to do, Flavia. It was the most difficult step I had ever taken in my life. But I could hardly leave the burden of everything on a woman. There is something in a man that balks at that. So I took the bull by the horns and walked up to the cannon's mouth. And now I am glad I did. It has smoothed the way."

"So your better side is very good, my boy," said Mr. Clare.

"Oh, well, yes, perhaps. Well, I suppose there was an element of something above the average about it. These things are in us when the demand comes. We find there is something there that responds to a call. Otherwise I don't see much point in maintaining a high moral tone. I would rather have an ordinary person who could come out under a test, than one of your paragons who say and do nothing wrong from morning to night. The little, everyday qualities don't bear much on deeper things."

"Do normally well-conducted people fail under a trial?" said his wife.

"Oh, I daresay they do. I have known it. And, what is more, you are failing under one now. So there is an illustration. What other man would come back after an effort on this scale, the greatest he had ever made in his life, and meet such an attitude in his wife? I don't believe another. What do you really think of what I have done? You must have an opinion."

"I think it may have been the best thing. And I see it was a magnanimous one. But perhaps it was rather premature. When did your first wife return?"

"To-day," said Cassius, using a full, easy tone, and causing it to swell as he proceeded. "An hour or two before I went to her. I told you I took the bull by the horns. What does that mean, if not that I acted at once? And any magnanimous impulse—any impulse has to be acted upon, if it is not to pass. I was afraid this would pass, I can tell you, as I strode along, trusting it would hold out until I arrived. I felt it ebbing away with every step. Premature? It was then or never."

"It was decided that it was to be never."

"And the decision has been altered, hasn't it? Or that was the trend of things. First I am looked on as a monster for keeping a mother from her children, and then there is this chill and hush because I try to put right any harm I have done. What is the good of abiding by mistakes? The right way to deal with them is to rectify them. If they are

80

to be sacred, what is wrong with them? Why are they mistakes? And what is to happen to the victims?"

"Have you no gossip, my boy?" said Mr. Clare. "Did not Catherine appear or move or speak? Is there no change in her after nine years? Did she not turn her eyes on you? It was her way to do so."

"Well, she is still a handsome woman," said Cassius, in a tone of interest in his words. "Her hair is going grey, but I think it suits her; I should say it does. I think it adds something to her that she seemed to need. And an older face fits her personality; it never added to her to be young. Oh, she still makes her own impression. I was not ashamed of once having seen her as I did. As for that brother and sister, I barely looked at them. I shook hands and did no more. Indeed I am not quite sure that I did that. I never liked them, and I am not going to begin. I can't think how she can have turned them out as she did. I thought better of her, I must say; well, better of her judgement."

"They have the name of being clever," said Flavia. "That does not give them a free hand."

"Doesn't it? I suppose you know, as you are hampered in that way yourself. Clever? They may be, if it is clever to be aloof and eccentric, and never say a word like anyone else. I declare, if either of the boys took after them, it would be a grief to me."

"When do you wish Catherine to meet them?" said his wife, in an even tone.

"Oh, it is 'Catherine' now, is it? In what spirit is that said?"

"I must call her something. What would you suggest?"

"I suggest nothing. You will decide for yourself. You never take my suggestions; so why ask me for them?"

"I will take one in this case, if you will make it."

"Well, I will not. I have none to make, as you know. You are only trying to harass me."

"I must arrange for them to meet in privacy and peace. It is a matter that needs thought."

"So it is, my dear; so it does," said Cassius, loudly. "And thank you for giving it. Thank you for doing your best for me. Thank you for always having done it. It smoothes this piece of awkward road for me, to have you at my side as a support. It is a queer sort of position for a man, to have to depend on one wife to help him deal with another. I declare I could laugh when I think of it." Cassius proved his words. "And I can't quite see how I have got into it. It does not seem to fit me somehow. I should have thought I should go through life in an ordinary humdrum way, and here I am situated as no man has been before or since."

"It was parting the mother and sons that led you to it," said Mr. Clare. "But you see it, and the matter ends."

"Then I am sure I hope it will do so. I am tired of this veiled carping and criticism, when I am trying to rise to the best that is in me. It needs an effort, I can tell you; and it does not do much to help a man, to have his wife and his father ranging themselves against him, as if they were part of the hostile world. He is prepared for the malice of mankind, but he looks for something else from them."

"It sounds as if your best was a good deal above your ordinary level."

"And so it is. And so is yours. And so is everyone's. Of course I know it is. The effort one has to make shows that. I only hope to be able to maintain it until the end. And now what is the end to be? We must think of that. Would it be best to ask Catherine to a meal in an ordinary, open way? It would seem more natural and less suggestive somehow."

"What of her meeting with her boys?" said his father. "Are our eyes to be on that?"

"Well, it has to be got through somehow. I don't know that they want to have it in a veil of darkness and mystery. Our being there might ease it for them."

"It would be a simple way to help," said Flavia.

"Yes, be ironic about it. I meant it in all good faith.

It might be the only way to do so. And I don't think sarcasm is quite the thing for the moment."

"You want to see the meeting, my boy," said Mr. Clare. "And we see your reasons; it will be a human scene; too much so for your wife and me. But what of the people most concerned? Would they not choose something else?"

"Oh, I don't think Catherine has much choice in the matter. She wants to meet her sons; the sooner the better, in public or in private; it is all the same. The main thing is the whole thing, if you understand me. There would be no trouble there."

"But we must do our best for her," said Flavia. "We have accepted her view and must act in accordance with it."

"Well, have the meeting in privacy then. Shut them all up together and leave them to work on each other, so that none of them is ever the same again. I am sure Guy will not be. If that is human kindness, have it like that. Of course your feeling for the boys is not that of a real mother. I see it could not be. And I see that it is not."

"I wonder what is best for all of them," said Flavia, in a detached tone.

"I do not wonder. I have told you my view. But I will not interfere. I will stand aside and see mystery made, and suggestions set on foot, and the boys' first impression of their mother constrained and spoiled. It is a strange thing to want to besmirch. Upon my word I should have shrunk from such an ordeal when I was a boy. And I have always thought of Guy as a more sensitive creature than myself."

"Well, what do you actually suggest?"

"I do not suggest anything. I know better than to do so. And I have already made my suggestion. I assumed that there would be luncheon as usual, and that Catherine would come to it in a normal way, and the children join us later, as they always do. Then everything would be simple and above-board, and no one would suffer. I hate the thought of unnecessary suffering myself. And the mother and sons could be alone together afterwards. Does not that cover the ground?"

"You make your case," said Mr. Clare.

"I suppose it does," said Flavia. "In a sense, of course it does. But is Catherine to wait until after the meal to see the boys? Is she to sit through an hour in suspense? We should do better for her than that."

"Well, let the boys come to luncheon. What is the objection there? Surely that takes in everything."

"We can hardly say it does not."

"You are making an occasion for yourself, my boy," said Mr. Clare. "And I don't say you deserve nothing."

"Well, and if I am," said Cassius, half-laughing, "I see no harm in it. I am sure we have one seldom enough. But my real object is to have this thing go through with the least possible strain, for you and for me and for Flavia and Catherine and everyone. And for the boys most of all. What is there to criticise in that? Why should we mouth and murmur over it, as though something discreditable were involved?"

"Well, will you suggest it to Catherine?" said his wife.

"Why cannot you write an invitation in the ordinary way? What is the reason for making any difference? There is nothing abnormal about the occasion. We are simply asking a woman to luncheon, who happens to have been involved in my life. That is all it is."

"Well, it is that amongst other things," said his father.

"She may answer that she wishes to see her boys alone," said Flavia. "It is what I should do in her place."

"But she will not, I tell you. Don't you listen to a word I say? You and she are not the same. God knows I understand you both. She wishes to see her sons, and nothing else counts with her. She does not mind how or where. That came through firm and clear. You see I know her well. Indeed it was extraordinary how things came back to me. All her little words and ways seemed to fit into their place as if we had parted yesterday. Or rather as if we had parted

84

when we were still on terms, you know. And to think that it is nine years, and that the three younger children have been born since! Well, how life goes by!"

"So it does," said Mr. Clare. "Mine has almost done so."

"I dread the effect of this meeting on the boys," said Flavia. "It is coming at the wrong age. They are at once too old and too young."

"Well, we can't help that," said her husband. "Just prepare them for it, as if it were an ordinary thing. They will soon adapt themselves."

"I see that you do not know them."

"And I see that you do not know me. I am always seeing it. You are too busy admiring yourself to have any admiration left over."

"So knowledge of you could only result in one feeling?"

"Oh, well, what do you say? Well, in what feeling? Oh, well, yes, you would take that line. Well, it might result in it. Or I think it might in this case. I do think there are things in me, that you don't recognise, Flavia. Just as no doubt there are things in you that I don't. But I recognise a good deal. God knows I do."

"Perhaps you read it in. That is an easy thing to do."

"Not for me. That isn't in my line. I only see that I can't help seeing. I don't want to see anything more. I am sure I don't. I guard myself against it. I don't want to know what is below the surface. It is advisable not to know it; I have found that. And now about this letter that has to be written. Ought we to make a draft?"

"Not if it is to be just an ordinary invitation. There should be no need. I suppose I address her as 'Mrs. Clare'?"

"Well, I suppose you do. It seems rather odd, somehow. And she will have to call you the same. So there will be two Mrs. Clares at the table. I might keep a harem."

"Well, not so much of one," said Mr. Clare.

"No, well, I suppose not. Well, I suppose I shall manage between them. I don't call either of them that; that is one thing."

"And a thing that will dispose of any problem," said his wife.

"And how about the children? Well, they don't call either of you that either. But what will they call Catherine?"

"Her own boys will call her 'Mother'. It is what they always called her. Fabian may just remember. The little ones will not use a name."

"Yes, that is why you were dubbed 'Mater'. I remember now. And I remember wondering why you liked it. It did not seem to suit you somehow."

"I did not like it. It did not suit me. It does not now. But the name, 'Mother', was given. It belonged to someone else. I did not take what was not mine."

"I remember; I do remember, Flavia. And I remember how you sunk yourself in other people and forgot your own claims. And I appreciated it, my dear; and I have appreciated it ever since. It is the foundation of our life together. Whatever else has been between us, we have that."

"Do you wish the letter to go to-day?"

"I don't wish anything about it," said Cassius, sitting down and throwing one leg over the other, as if threatened by exhaustion. "But, as I told you, Catherine wishes it, and it is she you are so concerned for. And if you had seen her all keyed-up and tragic, you would not keep her waiting a moment longer than you could help. No one would, who had a human heart."

"It is you who have kept her waiting for nine years," said Flavia, going to the desk. "She need not wait much longer."

"Well, upon my word, what a mean speech!" said Cassius, looking at her back. "Of all human meannesses give me that of a good woman. And when I say a good woman, I mean what I say. Well, what can we do to hurry things? Shall I leave the letter at the house?"

"No, that would be showing too much zest," said his father. "It is not a case for an excess of it."

"Simon can take it," said Flavia.

"And wait for an answer?" said her husband.

"I hardly think there is any need for that."

"Too much zest again? But, as I told you, if you had seen that woman, you would share my feeling. You would not expect me to consider what was due to myself. If you are what people think you, you would be shocked by it. You would not worry about zest. It is not a case for being concerned with convention. I declare I can't get her face out of my head. It keeps coming back to me."

"Well, Simon can wait for the answer."

"You are a good woman, Flavia, a woman sound at heart, if ever there was one. Your heart goes out to another woman in distress. You have no feeling about her coming to share your place. You are above it."

"Surely she will hardly be doing that."

"Well, we shall have her coming here, or the boys going there, or something of the kind happening. If there is to be this change, it will have to be managed somehow. I don't see any way out of it."

"I did not know the change was to involve so much. I understood there was to be a meeting, and I assumed it would be repeated at intervals, but not at frequent ones."

"Oh, you assumed that, did you? That is the knowledge of human nature of which you have so much! If I have any myself, the meetings will recur pretty often. What would you expect?"

"I expected what I said."

"Well, I expect something different. I have my own knowledge of life, and no mother who has been parted from her sons and then had them restored to her, would tolerate seeing them so seldom. It is not in human nature. You must know that. You are a mother yourself."

"To her children as well as mine, Cassius. It is the risk to them that troubles me. They cannot have two mothers."

"So that is what it has come to. I have heard you say the opposite. It seems that is what they will have. But there is surely no danger in it. The more mothers, the better, surely. We can't have too much of a good thing."

"The usual suggestion is that we can."

"Well, then they will have it. But it is better than too little. It is a fault on the right side. We must leave the future to itself."

"It holds more problems than you realise."

"Well, I can't help it, can I? I am sure I cannot solve them. I shall just let things take their course. And if you are guided by me, you will do the same. And you are guided by me more often than you think, Flavia. I am not such a nonentity in my own house. I often find my influence working and having its result. Though no one would acknowledge it. Oh, no, I should not expect that. But it remains that I am the head of the family, and that must mean something. Take the example of this last decision. Who really made it, you or I?"

"You had your own way," said his wife.

"And what is that but the same thing in other words? If I carry my point, my advice is taken; there is no way out of it. And here we have the answer to the letter. It is a good thing the boy was told to wait. That was a good idea of yours, Flavia. Well, I wonder what Catherine says. It is odd, but I have a queer sort of feeling of suspense."

"She will come," said his wife, laying down the letter.

"Oh, will she?" said Cassius, coming up and taking it. "I may read it, I suppose? Well, of course I may; it is written to us both; it is written to me more than to you really. Oh, it is just a formal acceptance in the usual terms."

"Well, what else should it be?" said Mr. Clare.

"The invitation was put in those terms," said Flavia.

"Yes, well, I suppose it was. You could not be expected to use any others, to show too much zest, as you would say. It is odd how her writing comes back to me. I might have seen it yesterday. I generally forget writings, and I don't think I saw it very much."

"I think it is natural that you should remember it."

"Yes, well, I suppose it is. I daresay she would remember mine, though she saw it even less. I don't often seem to write things, somehow. So it is at luncheon to-morrow that she will be here. And it is fourteen years since she came here first. What a thing it is to look back on the past!"

"A different thing for us all," said his father.

"Yes, well, I suppose it is. All men have their experience. And all women too, though we tend to forget that. So she took the first day that offered. She can't be unwilling to come. How did you put the invitation?"

"I gave her the choice of several days," said Flavia.

"And she took the first. Well, I was prepared for that. But she can't feel any reluctance to darken these doors. You might almost say she was showing zest."

"She is coming to see her sons. There is no sign of any other purpose. You realised her eagerness to see them."

"Yes, so I did. I read her mind. I seemed to see right into it somehow. I sometimes find myself doing that. Somebody's mind will lie right open before me. It is odd how we have these little individual powers. I suppose that is one of mine."

"It might be a dangerous one," said his wife.

"Yes, in the wrong hands. We have to remember what is vested in us. It is a sort of trust."

"What of your plans for to-morrow?" said his father. "You will be wise to give your minds to them. How will you sit at the table? There should be no uncertainty."

"Cassius and I in our usual places," said Flavia. "And Catherine opposite to you, with the boys on either side of her."

"Yes, well, she can't sit in her usual place," said Cassius, with a little laugh. "In her old place, I mean. But it will be the first time she has sat at the side of the table in this house. I wonder if she will think of it."

"She will probably be thinking of other things," said Flavia. "She certainly will, if you are right in your account of her."

"Well, my impression was what I told you. As I said, it all seemed quite clear. But I shouldn't be surprised if a thought of it goes through her mind."

"It would hardly be more than that."

"No, well, I suppose not. I expect I was right in my impression. Well, I wish the occasion was over. It gives me an odd, unsettled feeling. I never thought to sit at the head of my board, with one wife opposite to me, and another at my side. Well, I suppose I had my ways with women when I was young. It seems that I must have, though I did not give much thought to it. It has never been my habit to turn my eyes on myself. I just went on in my natural way."

"As you continue to do," said his father.

"Well, I wonder how the situation will develop. I can't help wondering how it will grow and spread, and make a difference in all our lives."

"To a certain extent," said his wife. "Probably to a great and growing extent. It is too soon to say."

"Yes, that is what I thought. You see how we really take the same view. We do that more often than you realise. Well, I am glad the occasion is upon us. The longer it is postponed, the oftener I shall live it in my mind. Catherine coming into this room! Well, I have seen that often enough. And I was glad enough not to see it any more at one time. I can tell you that I was."

"It is not our moment. It is hers and her sons'. I wish we could keep apart from it. As you know, I would have arranged to do so."

"Well, you came round to my view in the end. As I say, you often do. And we could not keep aloof beyond a point. We shall have to countenance the new condition of things. Well, I shan't be able to help picturing the scene. You see, to me it is not the same as it is to you. To me it is the last of many."

"And to us all the first of many more," said Mr. Clare.

CHAPTER VII

"Is it permitted to be glad to see you again, ma'am?"

"It is kind of you, Ainger. You are very little changed."

"It can seem as if an intervening chapter had not been written, ma'am."

"It may for the moment," said Catherine.

"As you say, it is erroneous, ma'am."

Ainger led the way to the drawing-room with a silent tread, and withdrew without making an announcement. It did not occur to him to treat the occasion as a normal one.

"Well, Catherine, so here we all are before you," said Cassius, coming forward. "You can form your own judgement of everything. It is all open to your eyes. There has been no preparation for your coming. There is nothing to hide."

His words died away as he ended. It seemed they would have been better not said. The scene did not need his direction; it would take its own course.

Catherine advanced with her quick, short steps, greeted her hosts without glancing at her sons, and turned and embraced them, with her eyes going openly over their faces. When she gave them her second glance, she was careful to give an equal moment to each. She sat down with their hands in hers, but released them as though fearing to be burdensome. Mr. Clare and Flavia kept their eyes from the scene. Cassius stood with his on the ground, but now and then raised them and surveyed it. Not a word was said; it seemed that no one could speak. A chance movement made a sound and brought relief.

Ainger announced luncheon in a low tone, that suggested it was an unsuitable necessity of the occasion. The move to the dining-room seemed at once a liberation and an exposure. Cassius gave some directions in his usual tones, and Guy looked up as if startled by them. Catherine sat between her sons, and remained calm and aloof, as if she were already satisfied. When they were questioned about their meal, she hardly looked at them, leaving the matter to their stepmother.

"Well, this is the first time the boys have joined us at luncheon," said Cassius.

"It is time they did so," said his father. "It ought to have entered our minds."

"What does their own mother think?" said Cassius, in a tone of taking a step that would have to be taken.

"I have not the experience that would enable me to judge," said Catherine.

"Flavia is a sound arbiter of such things."

Catherine's silence somehow gave full consent.

"Now do you find them much altered after all these years?"

"As much as I thought to find them. I should have recognised Fabian. Guy was only two when I left."

"Well, they have not wanted a mother," said Cassius, more loudly. "Have you ever wanted a mother, boys? Can you honestly say you have felt any lack in your lives?"

"We have always wanted one in a way," said Fabian, rising in his turn to an effort that was before him. "We always knew we hadn't one. Mater always let us know. But she has been the same to all of us."

"She has indeed. That is a thing that does not need saying, and that you are right to say."

"I used to wonder, when I first knew about things, if she would get tired of it. But she never did."

"Now there is a tribute, Flavia. What woman could ask more than that?"

Flavia heard her husband with her eyes down.

"But that kind of stepmother makes you wonder about a real mother," said Fabian.

Catherine also looked down and silence followed.

"Well, Catherine, how about your brother and sister?" said Cassius. "Do you find much change in them?"

"No, very little. They are nine years older and nothing more."

"Yes, that is what I thought. Nine years older and nothing more," said Cassius, somehow giving the word another meaning.

A faint sound of amusement came from Fabian, and Catherine smiled at him and looked away.

"I declare he is like you, Catherine," said Cassius. "I caught it at that moment when you both smiled. There was a definite flash of resemblance."

"You used to say we were alike. I could even see it myself. And I think I see it now."

"And Guy? Do you see any likeness in him?"

"No. Neither to you nor to me."

Flavia looked up at the coupling of the words.

"I suppose some ancestor accounts for him," said Cassius. "There is a portrait in the hall that is like both him and Tobias, our youngest boy."

"I see likenesses in all of them to their parents and each other," said Flavia.

"Yes, my wife is a great person for giving equal attention to all. What is done for one, is done for the rest. You can be sure of that."

"I am sure of it," said Catherine.

"Now what about the question of Fabian's going to school? We feel he is getting too old for this life at home. So he is only to have another year of it."

"I did not know there had been any question."

"It does not sound as if there had," said Flavia.

"A year is a long time," said Guy.

Catherine looked up, arrested by something in the tone.

"Could they not go together?"

"I fear they could not," said Flavia. "There are two years between them."

"Would not anything be better than a parting?"

"Nothing would be worse than a breach of convention," said Cassius. "You don't know a boy's world."

"No, I do not," said Catherine.

Guy looked from his mother to his stepmother, and in a moment looked again.

"Well, Guy, are you weighing the difference between them?" said Cassius, in a tone that somehow addressed the company. "You are a fortunate boy to have two mothers. So far from having less than other boys, you have twice as much."

A faint laugh from Catherine seemed to carry a load of memories.

"Well, that was the line of the boy's thought. And I declare he sets us an example. He is behaving in a natural manner, and I don't blame him. We cannot go on in this stilted fashion, behaving as if we had something to be ashamed of. It gives a false impression of our family life, and of the atmosphere in which the boys have been brought up. Now, Fabian, can you honestly say that this is our usual situation?"

"No, but the thing that is happening is not usual."

"And you think it justifies the change?"

"Well, I think it makes it natural."

"And what do you think, Guy?"

"I think it does too."

"Ah, it is a great occasion for you. A unique moment in your lives. A great many people live and die without an experience on this scale. You will be able to think and talk of it when you are a man."

"I don't think we shall ever talk of it, except to each other," said Guy, with tears in his voice.

"Now whatever is it?" said his father. "He is a strange child, Catherine. One never knows what is in his mind. Do you know what it is, Fabian?"

"He doesn't know which mother he belongs to most. He doesn't know which he should like the best. He can never be sure about things."

"Oh, that is it, is it? That is it, my poor little son. Come to your father," said Cassius, drawing the boy to his side and continuing with his arm about him. "Father knows what you feel. But things will settle themselves. You need not worry about them. Just take your feelings as they come. They will alter and take their shape. You are not responsible for them. Take each day by itself."

"There are so many days," said Guy.

"But only one at a time. 'Sufficient for the day is the evil thereof.' You must remember that. Well, what have I said now? What is there for you all to laugh at? I shall be afraid to open my mouth. And that will be a pity, as it seems that no one else can do so."

"Two mothers should be sufficient for any day," said Flavia, "when it is the usual provision for two lifetimes."

"Well, I can't tell you which to like the better, my boy," said Cassius, relinquishing his son. "Not even Father can do that. Just love them in different ways; that is my advice."

"You love Mater better," said Catherine, in a low tone. "Because she is the mother you know. Because she will always be the mother you knew first."

"Yes, I do now. But perhaps I shall get to know you."

"Take each day as it comes," said his father again. "That is the only thing."

"Guy could never do that," said Fabian.

"And neither could I," said Flavia. "Life is not a matter of days. Each one is a part of the whole."

"Well, everyone knows that," said her husband. "Why state such a thing as if it were a philosophic truth?"

"The separate days, rooted in the past, carrying the future," said Catherine, as if to herself.

Guy looked again from her to Flavia, and the latter caught his eye and gave him a smile. He relaxed with a sigh, and Catherine saw the interplay and smiled from one to the other.

"Well, it seems a happy occasion enough," said Cassius,

with his eyes on them. "I don't see anything sad or sinister about it. Does anyone? Do you, Fabian?"

"No, but I think it ought to have a description of its own."

"Well, how would you describe it?"

"Well, it is one I have always imagined. And it does what we wanted for us. We are getting to know. . . ."

"Mother," said Flavia, in a full, kind tone. "That is what you will call her. It is what you called her from the first. That is why I was called 'Mater', if you remember."

"We do remember, my dear," said Cassius. "And it has become a title of honour for you. We all recognise it."

"Is it better to be called 'Mother' than 'Mater'?" said Guy.

"Which would you choose?" said his stepmother.

"Well, they both mean the same thing. I think 'Mater'."

"That has the meaning for him," said Catherine.

"Which would be your choice, Fabian?" said his father.

"It would depend on what was the custom. It is that that makes the difference."

"Yes, it is that," said Catherine.

"But your sacrifice is not wasted, Flavia," said Cassius, loudly. "No honest sacrifice ever is. It has its own meaning for you, and so for other people."

"I doubt if the one follows from the other. It seems to me that it may be wasted. But it was not very great."

"But it was nagging and insistent," said Cassius, in a tone that seemed to fit his words. "Striking you where it made you shrink and shiver, at every turn! But it won you your husband's gratitude."

"Fabian remembered his mother. Some decision had to be made. I daresay it was the right one."

"It was, my dear, it was; the one that took no account of yourself. That is always the right one."

"I remember her now," said Fabian. "As she was when I first knew her, or as I thought she was."

"Well, well, the years have gone by since then," said

Cassius. "Look at the difference they have made in you. They can't pass over other people. They have not passed over your father."

There were sounds outside the door of the approach of the younger children. After the interval necessary for Eliza to set Toby down and insist on his entrance, it opened to admit them. Henry and Megan, with an air of following directions, came up and shook hands with Catherine. Toby stood still and surveyed her.

"Shake hands with Mrs. Clare," said Cassius.

"No," said his son.

"Is she Mrs. Clare?" said Henry.

"You heard what was said," said his grandfather.

"I thought Mater was that."

"So now you know the whole, my boy."

"Father and Henry both 'my boy'," said Toby.

"Come, do what Father tells you," said Cassius.

"How do you do?" said Toby into space, making a movement of shaking hands.

There was some mirth, and he appeared to search his memory.

"Quite well. Thank you. Fine day," he said, and turned and looked at Catherine.

"Lady," he said, in a tone of suggestion, and turned away.

"Ought he not to do as he is told?" said Cassius.

"He ought to be what he is," said Catherine.

"Ah, you missed those stages in your children, Catherine. That is what you are thinking of. I can read your mind like a book. It lies open before me. But they have wanted for nothing. You could have done no more for them."

"I could have had more from them."

"Well, well, that can't be helped now. You must just forget it."

"Forget it?" said Catherine, just audibly.

"Now they are older, they have more need of you."

"I have need of them. I must be on my guard."

97

"Well, let them speak for themselves. Now, Fabian, would you rather have one mother or two?"

"I would have chosen always to have my own. But as things are, I see I want them both."

"And you, Guy?" said his father.

"He wants the mother he has always had. And he will always have her," said Catherine.

Guy suddenly rose and went to his stepmother and buried his face on her shoulder.

"Well, it is natural, my boy," said Cassius. "And we honour you for having the feelings. And we honour you for being able to show them. It is a thing not given to us all. Well, Flavia, you do not come out of it with nothing."

Guy was so far from honouring himself that he could not lift his face.

"What relation is she to us?" said Henry, indicating Catherine.

"No relation, my boy. She is the elder boys' mother."

"Why isn't she our stepmother, if our mother is theirs?"

"Mater has never been a stepmother to them. She has been a real mother."

"But I mean in a legal sense."

"Oh, you do, do you?" said Cassius, glancing at Catherine. "So you have come to that."

"It is not the same," said Megan. "Their mother isn't Father's wife. He can only have one at a time."

"Ah, they are a pair, Catherine. They write poems and do I don't know what. I don't know what to make of them sometimes. I can hardly believe they are my children."

"You said that Megan didn't write the poem," said Henry. "So it does seem strange that she is your child."

"Oh, it does, does it? That is what you would say. And what about you. Are you the natural child for me?"

"I don't think I am. We are too different."

"And where does all this difference lie?"

"Well, you don't know the truth about things, and I have always known."

98

"Well, give me an example of all this truth. You cannot have seen so mùch."

"I have seen some to-day, though it is supposed to be a day of happiness. Fabian's mother is here, and it makes him see he has never had her. And Guy doesn't know which mother is really his."

"Oh, come, two mothers are enough for anyone. I think they are fortunate boys."

"Yes, that is what you would think."

"You can see her feeling the truth," said Megan. "I mean Fabian's mother."

"Well, upon my word. This is what a parent has to face. You are fortunate to have missed some of it, Catherine."

"No, I am not fortunate."

"Well, no, I suppose you are not. But there are two sides to every question. And I don't think you will have this sort of thing with Guy. He doesn't seem so full of it somehow."

"You always say he is backward," said Megan.

"Well, I am sure I ought to be glad of it. It is a fault on the right side. If I ever found any fault with it, I retract what I said. Give me a natural child."

"You haven't found out you like him as he is, until he has his mother, and it doesn't matter," said Henry.

"Why, the better things are, the worse you make them. There is no sense in such forcing of things. Your words mean nothing. Well, well, my little son, come to your father. If you must bear the troubles of the world, you want his help, and you shall have it. You have chosen a hard course. I wish you had not, for your own sake."

Toby ran up and waited to be included in the attentions.

"Ah, you are a happy little soul. I cannot imagine two children more different. I declare it is odd to be the father of you both."

"How do you do?" said Toby, offering his hand. "Quite well; so glad; very much."

99

"He watches us," said Mr. Clare. "We should be on our guard. He will be bringing up what is forgotten."

"And he doesn't always understand," said Megan. "So he often makes things seem different."

"I hope he will not prove the most difficult customer of all," said Cassius.

"Very good boy," said Toby.

"Is it true that the child is the father of the man?" said Guy.

"You must ask Mother that, or Mater," said his father. "It does not matter which. You are a happy boy to have the choice."

Catherine and Flavia met each other's eyes, ready to speak but waiting for each other. Flavia seemed the more resolutely silent.

"I think there is something in us, that remains in us and grows with us," said Catherine to her son. "That is what the words mean."

"So Mother knows," said Cassius. "There are two people who will always know, Mother and Mater."

"Mother," said Fabian, flushing as he spoke, "will you always come here to us, or shall we sometimes come to you?"

"Well done, my boy!" said Cassius. "You have taken the plunge. You have crossed the Rubicon. It will never be so hard again. It is a great thing to be able to surmount the obstacles in life. It will be easier for you in the end. Now, Guy, see if you can follow your brother's example."

Guy looked up as if in question.

"Say something to Mother and use that name. Then the step will be behind. And you will not be haunted by a sense of something to come, something that would get more difficult with every day."

"I can't think of anything to say."

"Oh, come, you cannot expect me to believe that."

"I believe it," said Megan, "because it is the truth."

"Oh, dear, oh, dear!" said Henry, looking from Guy to his father. "Trouble is made on purpose."

"You should prove your position, Cassius," said Flavia. "Say something yourself."

There was a pause.

"Well, I declare I can't think of anything. I declare that I can't. I should not have believed that words could dry up like that."

"You will now have a wider range of belief."

"Now you are an ill-natured little woman. Trying to make an exhibition of your husband. What I said to the boy was said in all innocence. There was no spite in it."

"Ask Mother if she has ever had the experience," said Flavia to Guy. "Say 'Mother, so you find it difficult to think of something to say on the spur of the moment?' "

Guy repeated the words in a quoting tone, and Catherine answered at once.

"Yes, I think it is a common thing."

"Well, it seems you are indebted to me for the thing to say, after all," said Cassius, in his grim manner. "It was I who put it into your heads. You did not think of anything yourselves. A common thing! It seems to be."

"Did you ever love Fabian's mother best in the world?" said Henry.

"Whom does Toby love best in the world?" said Cassius, keeping his eyes from one son and lifting the other. "Tell Father who it is."

"Mother," said Toby, in a reverent tone.

"Do you not mean Mater?"

"Oh, no."

"Why do you love her so much, the lady the boys call Mother?"

"Toby call her Mother too. Fabian and Guy and Toby. Poor Mother only come to-day."

"You really love Mother and Father the best."

"Oh, no, here to-day and yesterday."

"You little good-for-nothing! So new brooms sweep as clean as that."

Toby looked at him without comprehension.

"Do you love Mother better than Bennet?"

"Love Mother and Bennet."

"And no one else?"

"No," said Toby.

"The age of innocence!" said Cassius, as he released his son. "It ought to be called something else."

"Innocence seems to mean a good many things," said Megan.

"Well, you are all too much for me. So this is what it is to have a family. Whom do you and Henry love best in the world?"

Henry and Megan looked at each other and looked away.

"Come, answer a simple question."

"They have answered it," said Flavia, "and it was more than it deserved. That kind of question need not be answered."

"Why, I meant it in all innocence. What have I done now? Upon my word, I am an ill-used man. I wonder if anyone has any love for me. I should be surprised if no one has, after all I have done for everyone."

"What have you done?" said Henry. "I don't mean you haven't done anything. I just meant I didn't know."

"Well, what a question! I shall not answer it. It is the kind of question that need not be answered."

"I think it is," said Flavia.

"It was meant in all innocence," said Megan.

"Oh, was it?" said Cassius. "And is that meant in innocence too? I will not ask you if you love your father. I have had my answer."

"You know that is not true," said Henry. "Megan was making a joke."

"Oh? A joke is supposed to amuse us, isn't it?"

"I think it did amuse people."

"Well, Toby," said Cassius, as if he did not hear, "you will say something kind to Father."

Toby submitted to be lifted and waited to earn his release.

"Do you think about Father at all?"

"Oh, yes," said Toby, beginning to descend, as if his duty was done.

"How much do you think about him?"

"Very little bit," said Toby, with affection for the diminutive.

"And whom do you think about a great deal?"

"Bennet. No, Mother."

"But you have known her for such a little while."

"Very little while," said Toby with appreciation.

"Upon my word, Catherine, you have chosen the better part. The less you do, the more you get, it seems to me."

"It does not seem so to me, who have been able to do so little."

"Megan didn't say she didn't love you," said Henry to his father. "It was you who said it. There is no need to make things different."

"I think we know how they are," said Cassius, putting his arm lightly about his son, as if he had learned better than to go further. "But thank you, my boy. Father knows what you mean."

"Shall we go to the drawing-room?" said Flavia, rising from the table. "The children do not come with us, but the boys may like to to-day."

"Well, how do you feel, boys?" said Cassius, with a faint sigh in his tone.

"I should like to come," said Fabian.

"And that means that Guy would too. I know you speak with one voice, or that he speaks with yours."

"I will go now," said Catherine, standing straight and still. "It is enough for one day. I find it is enough. I go with a mind at peace. I go in gratitude. I shall be grateful for anything more that I am given."

She kissed her sons and went to the door, followed by

Cassius. Flavia held out her hand to Guy, and he came and put his into it. Fabian came and stood in front of them.

"I am not ungrateful, Mater. You may think I am. I shall never be," he said, speaking in short, quick sentences like his mother. "I have wanted this thing in my life. The thing the younger children had. I am glad to have it. But I know what you have given me. And I know you sometimes found it hard. I wanted the person who found it natural. But you will come third in my life. You will come after my mother and Guy. It is not much return for what you have done. But I shall not come so high in yours."

Flavia put her arm about him, and Cassius returned to the room, having been succeeded by Ainger in the hall. His eyes dilated coldly on what met them.

"Now, boys, you may run away," he said, his voice not disguising that he had had his fill of emotion. "You have stood up to the occasion. You have borne yourselves well and made your father proud of you. And now you may be your natural selves again. It is what he wishes for you."

The boys withdrew and Cassius threw himself into a chair.

"Well, I declare I feel that virtue has gone out of me. It was an exacting occasion, but I think I rose to it. I think I steered everyone through. And that was my part. What would both of you say?"

"It is difficult to talk about some of it," said Flavia.

"Yes, Fabian behaved like a man. I declare I was proud of him, and I should think Catherine was too. And I hope you were, Flavia. He did you credit, my dear. No mother could have done better for him. His own mother must have felt it. And I think she did, and meant to show it. I know her in those ways, and she gives people their due. Well, so you think it passed off well?"

"In the sense that we did our best in it. We could not do more, and so I suppose it could not have been better. Fabian has thought about things more than we knew. I ought to have realised it."

"No, you ought not. You ought not to have done any

more than you have. You have done everything, my dear. You have done too much. And you will not get much return for it, as far as I can see. It is a good thing you have children of your own. If you had not, you would be in a sorry place enough. But as it is, you will get your reward in your own way."

"I would choose the ordinary way. Just as the boys would have chosen the ordinary things."

"Guy would have chosen what he has had. He has made that clear, and it is fair to him to accept it. And Catherine accepted it openly; I thought she came out well there, Flavia. It was never her way to fail under a test."

"She behaved like an honest woman. We have always known she was that."

"She was; God knows she was," said Cassius, in another tone. "I have reason to remember her honesty. I remember the level we lived on. There was no getting away with little, every-day pretensions with her. One was always stripped of everything but the stark, staring truth. And there is an inner core in everyone that hardly bears that."

"It is true that cores are naturally hidden."

"I am glad you agree with me. I am glad you are honest enough."

"It seems that honesty is a common quality," said Mr. Clare.

"Honesty of a kind," said his son, grimly; "honesty directed towards other people. It is not often that we turn it upon ourselves."

"I should have thought that Catherine was more likely to do so than most of us," said Flavia.

"Well, perhaps she is. But she wants everyone to be subject to the same scrutiny. And people have a right to a choice in the matter, as in any other. Well, well, I suppose we are all acting. Not that I think I act overmuch. I think I am a natural sort of man. I don't often turn my eyes on myself."

"Mrs. Clare!" said Ainger, throwing open the door.

Catherine came forward, stood still and began to speak.

"I have returned. It is against my will. I could not do anything else. I have lost control of myself. I have been given much. I have come to ask for more. To ask to see my sons daily, hourly, when I wish, when they wish. I have come to ask for everything."

"Ah, you know the quarter to go to for that sort of thing, Catherine," said Cassius, as Catherine turned to his wife. "It has not taken you long to find that out."

There was a pause, and then Flavia spoke in a new tone, that still seemed to belong to herself.

"I cannot give you everything. You must know that no one should ask that. It leaves the other side with nothing, and that cannot be accepted. The boys must see this house as their home; they must see me as its head. Anyone who comes to it, comes as my guest."

"I will come as your guest," said Catherine.

"You would come as your children's mother."

"What else am I to them?"

"Many things. Among them a stranger."

"And what are you to them?"

"Many things. Among them a mother."

"You could remain a mother to them."

"You know I could not, and that you would not remain a stranger."

"You did not desire me to remain so."

"I did and do desire it, to the point where you have given your word."

"I am breaking it. I do not deny it. I have not strength to keep it."

"You cannot take that cover. You had strength to give it. You must have counted the cost."

"Come, come, let the matter settle itself," said Cassius, flushing and coming forward as if to separate two combatants. "Leave it to the future."

"I will not," said his wife. "It would mean that I had no future. My home is to be my own, and the children mine. Other people's word may not count, but mine stands as what it is. The boys may see their mother, know her, feel her influence. That is much to ask of me. I was told it would never be asked. Words, as I say, have no meaning. So I must protect myself. The more I give, the more must be given. Things must stop somewhere. I must cease from giving."

"Few people can stand power," said Catherine.

"What of yourself when you had it?"

"I had none. I sought your mercy."

"What is that but using power? There is no strength like pitifulness. And I have no more mercy. I have given what was in me."

"I do not think you know yourself."

"You mean you thought you knew me, and find your mistake. You did not judge me truly. I do not ask nothing for myself. You who ask everything, should understand that."

"I ask it again," said Catherine.

"And again I refuse it. I give you no hope."

Catherine turned and left the room, and left a silence.

"Well, well, well," said Cassius, "so it has come to this. And after it had gone off so well. I thought it seemed too good to be true. Well, I don't blame you, Flavia. I don't know that anyone is to blame. I daresay even Catherine was helpless."

"I daresay she was. So am I."

"Well, yes, I believe you are. So there is a deadlock."

"No there is the agreement between us, the conditions that were laid down."

"Well, it sounds reasonable, Flavia. I can't say it does not. And I thought you came out well; I was grateful to you. But I can't help being sorry for Catherine. I admit that I can't."

"I feel inclined to congratulate her. She has asked for much and obtained it, and has gone on to ask for all. I am not sorry for people who do that. They can serve themselves."

"Well, you have never done it, I admit. But your standard is too high for everyone."

"I see that it is. I must cease to observe it. It means that I stand alone, giving away what is mine."

"Well, well, it does seem like that. And so I suppose it is settled. Catherine comes and goes at your charity and discretion. And I know you can be trusted to use them both. There are the children in the hall. How they always seem to be everywhere! They should be able to give as well as take. We will call them and let them distract us."

"It will be well to let something do so," said Mr. Clare, who had stood in silence. "And they should have learned the business."

"So Toby has come to see Father," said Cassius, taking this line with a touch of weariness.

"Come and see Mother," said Toby, providing no diversity and looking round.

"It is raining," said Henry, giving his explanation of their presence.

"Where are Fabian and Guy?" said Flavia.

"They wanted to talk by themselves. I think things have got worse for them."

"I am afraid they have. Their life is simple no longer."

"It seems best to have your own mother all the time, or not to have her at all," said Megan.

"Having two takes all your thought," said Henry, "so that you don't have any over for your own life."

"I am afraid you see the truth," said his mother.

"Truth has to be seen, when it alters everything."

"Try and sight a favourable truth," said Mr. Clare. "You should cultivate a sharper vision."

"I can't think of one just now."

"So you liked the lady who came to-day," said Cassius to Toby. "But she likes Fabian and Guy better than you."

"Oh, yes, poor Guy! No, like Toby."

"Would you like to go and live with her?"

"Yes."

"And leave Father and Mater and Bennet?"

"Bennet come too. Bennet and Megan and Toby."

"And no one else?"

"Only William," said Toby, getting off his father's knee.

"Would you like to leave us all, Henry?" said Cassius.

"Well, you would not mind if I did."

"What a thing to say! Of course I should mind. Father would not know what to do without his little son. Wouldn't you mind leaving him a little?"

"Well, then I should, or else it would be sad for you. And there wouldn't be anywhere for me to go."

"And no one else would pay for our food," said Megan.

"Well, that is a reason for staying," said her father, drily.

"I suppose Fabian and Guy's mother would pay for theirs," said Henry.

"We do not talk about who pays for things," said Flavia.

"Who would mind paying for Toby's food?" said Cassius, not bearing out his wife's words.

"Pay?" said Toby, raising his eyes.

"Give money for it."

"Bennet does," said Toby, with a clearing face. "In a shop. Then Toby eat it."

"What does Toby eat?"

"Very nice bun. Henry and Megan and Toby."

"Does Toby have the biggest?"

"Oh, no, dear little bun."

"Does William have a bun too?"

"No, very nice beer."

"What do you like best to eat?"

"Only bacon," said Toby.

"Surely he does not have that?" said Cassius.

"He likes the smell of it," said Megan. "And he may have tasted it."

"Always eat bacon," said Toby.

"You should say what is true," said his father. "You know you do not have it to eat."

"No, not good for him, poor little boy!"

"A child is a strange thing," said Cassius, as they were left alone.

"It is a natural thing," said his wife. "That is why it strikes a civilised person as strange."

"Yes, well, I suppose one is a civilised person," said her husband, on a faintly gratified note, "though one does not think of oneself in that way. I suppose one's training and background have done their work. Well, Flavia, what is your impression of Catherine, now you look back on her?"

"I think it must still be based on yours. I have heard so much and seen so little, and seen that under strange conditions."

"Well, I can hardly tell you my impression," said her husband, leaning back and frowning, "though it sounds an odd thing for me to say. You see, I knew so much, or thought I did, but now that I see her, I am not so sure. And then I suddenly see I was right, and then I am in doubt again. So it is difficult to tell."

"It must be," said his wife.

"That is why I wanted to know what you thought. You must think something. And I can see that you do."

"I should say she is an honest, deep-natured woman, but of a purpose so single that it blinds her to any claim but her own. But that might be true of many of us in her place. What she is in her life I have had no chance of judging."

"And upon my word I can't tell you, though I lived with her for five years. More than half as long as I have lived with you, Flavia. And I feel I know you in and out, every corner and cranny of you. There is no question about you that I could not answer."

"I wonder which of them has the advantage," said Mr. Clare.

"Well, do you know, I think Catherine has. She is able to take cover under a veil of mystery, and never face the light of day, as Flavia does, and as I do myself in a way.

I declare I should like to let in the light on her inner self and turn my eyes on it."

"We should fear to do that to anyone. And you took exception to her doing it to you."

"Well, so I did, and so I do, or so I should, if it happened again. But mine is an ordinary, everyday self enough. It is hers that baffles one and gives rise to all sorts of problems. My little poses would be the usual ones. It is her great, unpitying penetration that hits you in the face and tricks you into betraying what is hardly there. I declare I used to reveal things that I did not know were in me or anyone. She used to open up a new, dark world to me. Her seeming to read my mind never resulted in my thinking more of her. Oh, it was an experience, I can tell you, living with her for five years. I have never been the same man since. You have never known me as I was, Flavia, and that has been hard on you as well as on me. Oh, people like Catherine do their own harm, in spite of their lofty stand. And she could not do with me. Oh, no, I was too ordinary and commonplace for her. And the world had to know that. She could not keep it to herself. She had to leave me because of it. Is it any wonder that I imposed conditions on my own behalf? And yet I feel her influence and that odd sort of compelling force. It is a strange thing. Well, I don't know when I have had an outbreak like this. Do you remember my having one, Flavia? The past was somehow too much for me. It rose up and overwhelmed me. I did not foresee this result of having Catherine in the house."

"The past would be too much for any of us, if it did not stay in its place," said Mr. Clare.

"And now the future looms before us with all sorts of threats and doubts. Shall we ever be through it?"

"When we are through everything. But keep your thoughts away from it. You find the present enough."

"Of course I do, and so do you, and so does everyone."

"Well, it is enough," said Mr. Clare.

CHAPTER VIII

"Well, what is the news, Mr. Ainger?" said Madge.

Ainger crossed the kitchen with a slow tread and his eyes on the ground, and paused with his hand on his chair before he took his seat.

"News?" he said, raising his eyes.

"Yes. What is there to tell."

"There is nothing that asks to be told, Madge."

"We have suffered a sense of anticipation," said Kate.

"It pleases him to keep things to himself," said Halliday.

"I don't think thought of self has entered in," said Ainger, drawing in his brows. "There are cases where it does not."

"Are there?" said Mrs. Frost.

"Was it for nothing that Simon was excluded from the dining-room?" said Ainger, with more force. "Was it an indication or was it not?"

"We hope it was," said Madge. "What did it indicate?"

"That things were not for eyes and ears, except in cases."

"So did nothing happen?" said Halliday.

"Happen?" said Ainger, turning fully to him. "You would not expect incidents to take place?"

"I think we half expected it," said Kate. "Things might have given rise."

"The gentry are themselves," said Ainger, "as you are aware."

"So I was," said Mrs. Frost.

"Human beings like all of us," said Halliday.

"No, Halliday," said Ainger, gently, "not quite like that."

"Did the two ladies address each other?" said Kate. "That seems a salient point."

"You use the word, Kate. 'Ladies'. More is superfluous."

"What were you doing all the time?" said Halliday.

"What I could do. Being a friend to them in my own way."

"Well, be a friend to us in ours," said Madge.

"There must have been a good deal of waiting to be done," said Simon.

"Being a friend to them in their way," said Halliday.

"Well, that was my duty, Halliday," said Ainger, simply.

"England expects it of everyone," said Kate, sighing.

"Ah, we know it, Kate," said Ainger. "You are correct in your figure."

"There is a strain of what is higher in all of us," said Kate.

"But it is a pity it comes out in Mr. Ainger just now," said Madge.

"I suppress it in myself," said Mrs. Frost, "for fear it should be too high."

"I am sorry if you meant to make a Roman holiday of it," said Ainger. "It does not appeal to me in that light."

"Can you eat anything?" said Mrs. Frost, with her lips grave.

"Well, it has taken it out of me. It could not be otherwise."

"Well, when you have put it back into you," said Madge, "I hope we shall see the result."

Her hope was realised as far as could be expected. Ainger followed her suggestion, and then sat up and looked about him.

"Well, it was a human scene. Human nature was writ large. And it is a thing that makes its appeal. I have always been struck by it."

"But what was said and done?" said Madge.

"Nothing of a nature to be passed on. But much. It was a contradiction in terms."

"Well, tell us what you can," said Halliday.

"Greetings were exchanged," said Ainger; "remarks

were passed; convention was pursued. But there was nothing that made for disclosure. It was the outward and visible sign."

"Of the inward grace," said Kate.

"There is no better word. It is the one I should apply."

"Was there no sign of emotions underneath?"

"Kate, would signs have been in place?"

"Well, we rather feel they would," said Madge.

"The interchange might have marked any ordinary occasion."

"Perhaps that was what it was," said Mrs. Frost.

"You would almost have thought it, Mrs. Frost," said Ainger, turning to her frankly. "So complete was the effort made, and the success that crowned it."

"How did the master comport himself?" said Kate.

"Like himself," said Ainger, smiling. "There was the first hesitation, and then the torrent flowed. And it was opportune, as there was the silence of constraint."

"Did the former mistress extend marks of recognition to you?"

"Kate, we might have parted yesterday. I found myself looking to her in the old way. And the present mistress smiled upon it. I could have let the tears start to my eyes."

"Well, I expected to be more entertained and less uplifted," said Madge.

"You use the word," said Ainger. "I can feel the better."

"I should have liked to see the ladies in contact," said Kate. "It constitutes the climax."

"It was the high-water mark, Kate. As high as we need to go."

The bell rang and Ainger rose with a sigh and a movement of his shoulders, as if acquiescing in the continued need of him.

"It seems we have not always done justice to Mr. Ainger," said Kate.

"He has not always done it to himself," said Mrs. Frost. "I don't think he ever has before."

"I hope he won't make a habit of it," said Madge.

"We can tolerate anything the first time," said Halliday.

Ainger returned, resumed his seat and rested his head on his hand.

"Well, they soon spared you," said Halliday.

"Yes. Yes," said Ainger, just shaking his head. "There was not much I could do for them. I think it was just the glimpse."

"There was not time for much more," said Madge.

"I think I fulfilled their need, Madge."

It appeared that he was mistaken. A step sounded in the passage and Cassius came to the door.

"Ainger, this is not the wine I meant. I must come and show you myself. It seems impossible to get it."

Ainger rose with a finished, willing movement, hastened to the door to open it for his master, and preceded him to the wine cellar to do the same. Presently they were heard in the passage, Cassius using his ordinary tones, and Ainger subduing his, so that any subject could be inferred.

"No, I can take it myself," said Cassius, revealing the nature of the last one. "I am going back to the library."

Ainger returned with a firm step to his place.

"The master would carry the bottles himself," he said, smiling. "I did not want to be spared."

"Well, you had what you wanted," said Halliday.

Ainger gave him an absent smile and relapsed into thought.

"Are we allowed to disturb Mr. Ainger's reflections?" said Madge.

"Yes," said Ainger, looking at her kindly, "I am not so enamoured of them."

"Being to do with the family?" said Kate.

"Yes. The master did his best to give a natural impression. But I see that the heart is beneath."

"I have never seen him when he did not give one," said Madge.

"No," said Ainger, looking at her in gentle acquiescence.

"You think he would not show himself to me?"

"Now why should he, Madge?"

"I should certainly be flattered by it."

"Yes," said Ainger, looking into space. "One does feel that at first. But feelings supervene."

"You get your experience of life at second-hand," said Halliday.

"Yes. Yes," said Ainger, spacing his words and just raising his brows. "It does amount to that. I find I can identify myself. But you, if I may say so, do not get any at all."

"May you say so like that?" said Mrs. Frost.

"The real thing or nothing for me," said Halliday. "Do you not agree, Mrs. Frost?"

"Do you mean that I have nothing?"

"The appreciation of all of us," said Ainger, in a full tone reminiscent of his master. "Is that quite nothing? And I will tell you one thing, Mrs. Frost; and I don't often commit myself like this. If there was anyone I could find myself regarding as a mother, it would be you."

"Be a good son to me," said Mrs. Frost.

"Is the first Mrs. Clare still in the house?" said Kate.

"No," said Ainger, a smile playing on his lips. "I have attended her to the door."

"What is the jest?" said Halliday. "Is there some second meaning?"

"In a sense it was twofold," said Ainger, still smiling.

"You showed her out when the moment came."

"That may be said of me. There is the ground."

"In some double sense?"

"In one, if you like," said Ainger, yielding to a broader smile.

"Did you exchange any words?" said Kate.

"We stood in converse for some minutes. But exchange was hardly the term. I felt it was for me to stand silent."

"Did she ask after your welfare through all these years?"

"She did not fail to, Kate. And I answered her briefly, feeling that brevity was in place."

"We know more about you than we did," said Halliday.

"It is often possible to live with someone and not know much about him, Halliday."

"Especially if he forgets to tell us," said Madge.

"You none of you know what life implies," said Ainger.

"I don't think you have known very long," said Madge.

"Of course we know," said Halliday. "Birth and death have come to us all."

"Birth has come to me," said Mrs. Frost.

"It is the space between that comprises matters," said Kate.

"As I think the former mistress felt," said Ainger. "Indeed it was tacit between us."

"Well, I must admit to a sense of disappointment."

"Ah, you wanted to hear of incidents, Kate."

"It would have been nice," said Madge.

"But I should have been called upon to witness them. And that would not have been so. To see people of calibre fall from their level! But I was to be spared."

"I hoped to be called upon to hear of them," said Madge. "I wish they had something common done or mean, upon that memorable scene."

"The words apply, Madge," said Ainger.

"Who was it who did nothing common or mean?" said Simon.

"It was only once that it was anyone," said Mrs. Frost.

"Someone who was to be beheaded," said Kate. "It would be hard to be oneself then."

"Anyhow for long," said Mrs. Frost.

"It was Charles the First of England," said Ainger; "Charles, our Royalist king."

CHAPTER IX

FLAVIA LEFT HER home and went on foot to the house of the Scropes. She walked as though she wished to meet no one, but would not avoid doing so, as though her errand were not surreptitious but her own. She was taken to Catherine and began at once to speak, as if she knew her words by heart. The words seemed to have an echo of the other in them.

"I have come to say one thing to you. That I withdraw what I have said. It is as if I had not said it. You shall see your sons when you wish, as you wish, as often as you wish; at any hour or moment, in the day or in the night. I want to do my best for them, and this is my best. I should have known it, but for the moment I did not know. I have to do a mother's duty to them, and that is to give them to their own mother. I did not find it easy, and that may show they belong to you. Take them and do your part by them. I could not give up my own children. I will not ask you to give up yours."

"I knew you would not. I felt it in you. I saw it in your eyes. That is why I dared to ask everything from you, dared to hope for it when it was denied. That is why I can accept it from you, as a thing you have a right to give and I to take. I take it fully and gratefully as my right and yours. There are people from whom we can take. I shall remain in your debt willingly. I shall be willing to be unable to repay. I could not say it to everyone. I say it to you."

"I hope you will say anything to me, that you will ask me, tell me, anything you have to ask or tell. It is my wish to help you, answer you, take your help."

"I acknowledge my good fortune. I know it for what it is. It is a light across the darkness of my life, a break across its waste. I can see it in another light. And it is a relief to escape from bitterness. There is an especial sadness in self-pity."

"It is strange that we should be blamed for it," said

Flavia, in another tone. "As if we should feel it without cause, or desire to have cause for it. And we are allowed to feel pity for other people, even enjoined to. There is one rule for us and another for them. Self-love, self-pity, self-esteem are all terms of reproach. The only thing we may do is respect ourselves, and that seems to be compulsory."

"Well, the rules would have to be strict," said another voice, as a figure rose from the hearth and moved into view. "My sister and I are at home in talk of this kind. We were frightened by the other. We are afraid of the truth."

"And you are right," said Flavia. "It is a thing to be afraid of."

"But it is a mistake to be prepared for it. We never know when preparation may come in."

"Have you been there all the time?" said Catherine.

"We are always there," said her sister. "In summer or winter, by a warm hearth or a cold. I expect we are like crickets."

"You should not forget to chirp. That is your work in life. You have not met Mrs. Clare."

"We could hardly do that," said Elton, shaking hands. "But I have observed her from a distance and thought of her leading a life that was too much for you."

"That is the way to think of her. As someone who can do what is beyond other people."

"We have seen the nobler side of human nature," said Ursula. "And it is so much nobler; I had no idea of it. I am greatly softened. I hope it is wholesome discomfort."

"We can be cynics no longer," said her brother, "even though people will not think we are so clever. We must be true to our new knowledge."

"Do people think you are clever?" said Catherine.

"I think they must, when we have tried to make them. No real effort is wasted, and this was a real one. And perhaps we are, compared with them."

"Do we all regard ourselves as above the average?"

"Well, think what the average is."

"That hardly matters," said Flavia, "as everyone seems to be above it. Can you think of an average person?"

"Well, I would rather not think of one," said Ursula.

"Most people must be average," said Catherine, "or there would not be such a thing."

"Well, let us hope there is not," said her sister.

"I find them pleasant to look at, pleasant to listen to, pleasant in themselves."

"I am sure they are. But I do not find them so."

"There must have been times in your youth when you felt you were average or below. They come to us all."

"Do they? I did not know."

"Catherine, I hope you are not average," said Elton.

"I am the last person to object to being so."

"Then you are not, or you would object to it."

"Is there any meaning in anything we say?"

"Yes," said Ursula, "a dreadful, simple meaning. We look down on our fellow-creatures, and you are proud of not doing so."

"And do they look down on you?"

"Well, I don't see how they can."

"They may think you are eccentric and unlike other people."

"Well, I hope they think that."

"So you are sensitive to their opinion?"

"Yes, it is so high. I value it very much."

"You know you are quite inconsistent?"

"Yes, I know."

"You see very little of them."

"It would be a risk to see too much," said Elton. "Suppose they thought we resembled them!"

"So you work at maintaining the difference?"

"Yes, our life is a braver struggle than many that are more recognised."

"People do not suspect it," said Ursula. "They are too generous."

"Would you like anyone you had brought up, to turn

out like this?" said Catherine, smiling at Flavia. "It is time their sister returned to them."

"It is time for you to do so much. And I am to help you where I can. I am to work for your children under you."

"I say the same to you. I use the selfsame words."

"We have had the subject changed," said Elton to Ursula. "Could they have thought it was not a necessary one?"

"I wish I could say some noble thing. I feel them rising up within me, but I never know what they are. And I might be embarrassed if I did. What about our influence over the boys, if we see them?"

"I trust you," said Catherine, in a sudden tone. "Trust people, and they will be worthy of trust."

"So they are not worthy of it anyhow," said Ursula. "I wonder how far the principle works."

"Not very far," said her brother. "Distrust and watch people, and they will be worthy of it."

"I do not take that view," said Catherine. "I will not take it."

"I fear it has its truth," said Flavia. "For example, we used to think people would pay their debts, and now we refuse to lend."

"We give what we can," said Catherine.

"So your trust has quite gone," said her sister.

"We have to learn to give."

"It seems that we do," said Elton.

"You are both honest," said Catherine.

"Well, we like facing the worst. We recognise the hopelessness of things."

"And you appreciate it," said Flavia.

"Yes, other people cannot be too fortunate."

"It is something to feel that," said Ursula, "but I am afraid they can."

"Afraid is a very honest word," said Elton. "I am afraid some people are rich."

"Riches do not bring happiness. But I am afraid they do."

"And some have happy temperaments. There seems no end to it."

"Do you think that is true? Should we not sometimes meet them?"

"Believe it or not," said Catherine, "I had one when I was young."

"It is hard to believe," said her sister.

"Have you not happy temperaments yourselves?"

"Catherine, how can you?" said Elton. "Have you not looked into our eyes? We know they have their own melancholy, when we give it to them."

"What of your temperament?" said Catherine to Flavia.

"I have lost sight of it. It has long been overlaid."

"Perhaps ours have," said Elton. "I daresay that is it."

"I see mine has," said Catherine. "I must try to recover it. It is no longer only my own concern. That is a thing I have longed to say."

"Things do put you at such an advantage," said her sister. "We are never shown at our best. We hardly know what it is, and I don't think anyone else even suspects."

"I believe I know," said Elton.

"What is the good of an impulse to rise to heights, if it has to be wasted?"

"You want to do something noble?" said Flavia.

"It is not as bad as that. We only want to be known to have done it. Why should it be known about other people and not about us, when hardly anything is noble really?"

"You will tell me when I shall see you," said Flavia to Catherine, as she took her leave, "or if you wish to come without my doing so. It will be for you to say."

The two women went into the hall and talked for some time before they parted.

"So we ought to have left them," said Ursula, "but I am glad we did not. Virtue is its own reward, and we wanted another."

"Catherine is no longer a tragic figure," said Elton. "It seems unworthy of her. It is so ordinary for things to go well, though that is odd, when it is so unusual."

CHAPTER X

"WELL, THIS IS a nice position for a man," said Cassius. "Alone in the morning, alone at noon, alone until night! What is the good of a wife, when you never see or hear her? What is the good of having two wives, when they neutralise each other? I wonder there is a law against it, if it recoils on a man's head."

"You said you might keep a harem, my boy. I don't know how you would have managed with one."

"Yes, make a mock of me. It is what I expect. Leave me without a word of human kindness. I should be surprised by anything else."

"Then why be surprised by that?" said Mrs. Clare. "But you need not fear I will not serve you. It is the one way left to me to serve myself."

"It is a hard thing," broke out his son, "this emptiness in my home. Silence instead of a familiar voice, silence instead of a familiar step, silence, silence, silence, wherever I turn. Two women absorbed in each other like this! It is not a wholesome thing, apart from their being wives of the same man. It may set tongues to work."

"It is a long time since Catherine has been your wife."

"Well, she might almost be my wife again, now that she has a right in my house, or a right of way through it, or whatever it is she has. Whatever it may be, she makes the most of it. I am always encountering her, or her and Flavia together. I hardly dare to set foot in my own hall. They have no eyes or ears for anyone but each other. And I am left high and dry, with my children tossing a word to me out of pity. I wonder you like to see your son in such a plight. If I have no wife, I have the more need of a father."

"I wish I could meet the need, my boy. But my time is running out. I have reached my useless days."

"You might let fall a word to Flavia at some time. Unless you are afraid of her. I believe a man is always afraid of a woman."

"We should be afraid of anyone to whom we let fall a word. Hell holds no fury like such a person."

"And you would think I might say the word for myself, a great, strong man in the heyday of my life. But my soul shrinks up within me when I think of those two pairs of eyes in those two women's faces. I don't want to see the noble souls behind them. They give nothing to me; they only tear my own soul out of its place. What I want is a little normal fellowship in my middle age. I thought that Flavia and I would go down the years together, just as I thought it about Catherine. I am not a man to go alone through life. And I get a look or a word thrown to me out of their kindness. Kindness! It is a quality I have come to despise. If ever a man had enough of it, it is I. And you are looking at me as if you hardly saw me. I suppose I must expect nothing."

"You must expect it from me, my boy. I am past being of use. I have to ask for your help to me. It is true that I hardly see you. I am in need of the drug that helps me in my bodily decay. It is kept in the drawer of the desk. I am to take one tablet, as it is said that more would harm me. My days of labour and sorrow are to be prolonged."

"Do you take them more often than you did?" said Cassius, as he brought the flask.

"I am not at an age to take less. It is a palliative, not a cure. And as such I am dependent on it. Ten is said to be fatal to us. It is written on the label to protect us from ourselves, or other people from us."

"Isn't it dangerous to have such things about?"

"We do not do so. They are kept under cover. They are necessary in certain cases. You know that, when you are one of them."

"It would be an easy way of putting an end to oneself. Why are we not allowed to take our own lives? It seems that they are our own."

"We are seen as mattering enough to be forbidden to do so. I agree we should not expect it. Human lives are sacred, and we all have one. A poor thing, but our own."

"So I could end my life by taking ten of these," said Cassius. "And I might do so for all anyone would care. It would be a shock to people, I suppose."

"But you would not be here to see them suffer it. So it would be wasted."

"So it would in a way. I don't mean I want them to have it."

"Well, hardly enough to give your life for it."

"Oh, well, you have your own way of putting things. And I see it has a certain truth. But it is not the whole."

"A certain truth is our own truth, my boy. The whole seldom concerns us."

"This house would be a different place without me, though I am held to be of so little account."

"You would not see it in that state, however great a treat it would be."

"Oh, well, well, you are still yourself. We don't know what we shall be able to do in our future state."

"Would that be the sort of privilege afforded, things being as you would have them?"

"I only meant we might be granted a wider range."

"Dead men tell no tales, my boy. And they would do that, if they could do anything. And I doubt the advantage of seeing things going on without us. You see, that is what they would be doing."

"But in a different way."

"No, in the same way, but without us."

"You would miss me, if I were dead."

"It is you who will miss me. And I do not look to be flattered by it."

"I should miss you indeed, my dear old father. I could

not face life without you. I can imagine taking ten of these, to go with you wherever it is. And I cannot think it is nowhere. There would be no hope in anything, and we cannot live without hope."

"That may be our reason for contriving it."

"I wonder what Flavia would think, if I put an end to myself."

"No, it is not your solution. You want your reward, and you would not have it."

"There is not much to bind me to life."

"But no more to tempt you to lose it."

"It would be a good lesson for people, to have to do without me."

"If you have their improvement enough at heart to die for it."

"It would be a kind of revenge on them."

"Well, perhaps you might die for that, if you could see it."

"Why should I want that so much more?"

"Well, revenge is sweet, but it is not so true of people's improvement."

"I should like to see those two women's faces, if I were found cold and stiff in my bed."

"So it is as sweet as that. But you must give up hope. There is no way of arranging to see them."

"You must have death the end of everything. I believe we shall pass to a fuller life."

"And with your own kind of fullness."

"Well, I suppose we shall have passed beyond all personal feeling."

"It would be no good to take revenge, if you would not want it any more."

"You do not understand me. I was only using my imagination."

"Well, let it do the whole thing for you, my boy."

Cassius heard sounds outside the door and went to open it. Flavia and Catherine were crossing the hall, with the five children about them. Cassius stood and surveyed them.

"Well, are you all coming to say a word to your father?"

There was no reply.

"Or is no one coming?" said Cassius, in another tone.

Toby took a few running steps towards him and retreated. Guy looked from his stepmother to his mother and did no more. The other children gave no sign.

"I suppose they can recognise me when they see me. Anyone would think I was a stranger."

"No," said Flavia gently, "I think no one would think that."

"So I am a monster, am I?"

"You need not be that, to be difficult to approach."

"Now what a way to talk to me, a father such as I am! Have my children ever had a harsh word from me? If they have had a bitter one, whose fault has it been? Have they ever heard me raise my voice, seen me raise my hand? What would they say to an ordinary father, if I am seen like this?"

"Ordinary things are sometimes best in their place."

"No, they are not. That is a speech without a meaning. You have thought of it at this moment as something clever to say. Ordinary things are not as good as things above the ordinary."

"I said the best in their place."

"Things that are best in themselves, are best in any place," said Cassius on a triumphant note. "Quality must hold its own."

"Yes, you do well, my boy," said Mr. Clare, as he went to the stairs.

"Poor Father!" said Toby suddenly.

"Yes, poor Father!" said Cassius. "Toby's poor old father! But Toby loves him, doesn't he?"

"No. Oh, yes, poor Father!"

"And Father loves his Toby."

"Yes, dear little boy."

"And dear Father."

"No, dear Toby."

"Will you two elder boys come for a walk with me?"

"Yes," said Guy, approaching him.

"We were going for a walk with Mother," said Fabian.

"Well, which do you want to do?"

"Well, we had arranged to go with Mother."

"Did you know that, Guy?" said Cassius.

"No. Yes. Yes, I did."

"You are as bad as Toby."

"Or as good," said Flavia. "They both tried to give you what you wanted."

"Oh, I don't want scraps of attention thrown to me, as if I were a beggar in their path. What a way to regard their father! I am content to go my own way, communing with myself. It may be the best companionship."

"It is the only kind we can have," said Henry.

"Oh, you have found that, have you? You are in the same plight as I am. Alone amongst many, as is said."

"Yes, that is what it seems to be, though I didn't know people said it. Megan and I have found that our minds are different."

"How would you like to be really alone as I am?"

"You and Grandpa are together."

"Yes, that is what has to be said of me, a man with wives and children—a man with a wife and family."

"Isn't it a good thing for you to be with him?"

"Yes, indeed it is, my dear old father! It is the thing that binds me to life."

"I suppose he must die before long."

"Don't speak of it," said Cassius, putting his hand to his face, as though to ward off a danger, and sending his eyes to his wife behind it. "I could only wish to follow him."

CHAPTER XI

"Ah, Miss Bennet, we see you," said Halliday. "Open the door and come in to us. You must hear it all before you are at peace. Come in; we understand it."

Bennet seemed to wander to the table and stood absently fingering it.

"So nothing really happened," she said, the words seeming to fall of themselves from her lips.

Ainger, who was sitting with his chin on his hand, lifted his eyes.

"Nothing is not the word I should use," he said, and let them fall.

"Neither should I," said Halliday. "We need a different one. It is a slur on the house, the master stooping to this."

"That may not be the way to see it," said Kate. "It might argue a want in us."

"And no reason but discontent with a life that is better than ours."

"We have not the insight into things."

"I blame myself," said Ainger, seeming to stifle a sigh.

"Well, no one else blames you," said Halliday. "What was it to do with you?"

Ainger lifted his eyes and rested them on Halliday's face.

"My poor master!" he said, and said no more.

"And 'poor man', it seems."

"Yes," said Ainger, quietly. "There is no sting like self-reproach."

"Events cast shadows before. I ought to have foretold it."

"Foretold the actual thing?" said Bennet.

"Perceived the signs. They ought to have put me on my guard. It was in my power to disperse them, as I had done before. But I went on my own way, blind to his need. I have to say it of myself."

"You could not watch him as if he were a child," said Kate.

"It is what I have always done," said Ainger, almost giving a smile.

"Well, it was time you stopped," said Halliday.

"And it seems that he thought so," said Mrs. Frost.

"Does the master hold it against you?" said Kate.

"It is a question, Kate. I have asked it of myself. I seem to catch a look in his eye, that speaks to me and says I should have saved him from himself."

"He cuts a sorry figure," said Halliday.

"And he was prepared to leave his father desolate," said Kate, as if continuing the thought.

"Now that is what strikes one," said Ainger. "That is the dark point. The hearts of the two gentlemen are knit to each other. I should not have expected the pitilessness. Things were indeed too much."

"It seems there was intervention," said Kate.

"It does seem so, Kate. That he was frustrated by a higher hand. By his own he would have left us. It chanced that he resisted the fatal amount. The doctor would have been too late."

"His time had not come," said Kate. "So it is not for us to decide."

"He must be a strong man," said Bennet.

"I should hardly say so," said Ainger. "That is more for the outward eye. It vanishes with understanding. I should say I am the stronger of the two."

"Can't you think of yourself apart from him?" said Halliday.

"Well, we are not so often apart."

"You talk as if you had no work to do."

"He is the main part of it, and becomes more so. He knows it and keeps it in his heart. That is the real reason for Simon's presence."

"You expect to become knit closer?" said Kate.

"Or are arranging it," said Halliday.

"Well, nothing stands still in this world," said Ainger.

"It usually seems that everything does," said Mrs. Frost.

"How does Simon get on?" said Bennet, looking at the latter in experienced kindness.

"He shapes," said Ainger. "And that is all that is required at the moment."

"Until the master absorbs all your energy," said Madge.

"Until then, if you like."

"There will be a wound in Mr. Clare's heart that time will not heal," said Kate.

"Time won't have much chance at his age," said Halliday.

"To leave his grey hairs to go down to the grave!" said Kate, shaking her head. "Was it a son's part?"

"A son's part has been done," said Ainger. "I stand as a witness to it. Whatever has been left undone, it has not been that."

"Does the master love his father better than his wife?" said Simon.

"It is not for you to gauge affections," said Ainger, "or to introduce the family under relationships."

"On which side does your sympathy lie, Mr. Ainger?" said Kate.

"Kate, I will admit it. On the master's. It may not be the right one or the one favoured by the many, but it is mine. I follow an instinct. It is the guide."

"The mistress has done her best."

"And wholeheartedly I admit it. No one gives the mistress fuller credit than I. She has striven to her utmost. I am in a position to judge, as in a sense we work together."

"And what would you say for the master?"

"I would say nothing. There is nothing to be said. But the heart does not follow the head's dictates. My eye goes after him as if he were my child."

"He is old enough to be your father," said Madge.

"No, there is not so much between us. A matter of a dozen years. It is more the distance of an elder brother."

"That is not your basis," said Halliday.

"It is not," said Ainger, smiling. "I am rather in the position of the elder myself."

"And you are in another position too."

"And I hope I fulfil it, Halliday. I should think the less of myself, if I did not. And I ask no other. It is a position of trust."

"Then we are all in one," said Madge.

"Wholeheartedly I admit it, Madge," said Ainger.

"Perhaps my distance is that of an elder sister," said Mrs. Frost.

"Now we will not go through the whole gamut," said Ainger.

"Now that you have dealt with your own part in it."

"Well, I think I have a right to, Mrs. Frost," said Ainger, looking at her frankly. "It is one by itself."

"What is Simon's distance?" said Bennet, smiling.

"My words may apply in Simon's case, Miss Bennet," said Ainger.

"The children are fonder of the mistress than the master," said Kate.

"I endorse it, Kate. And it is true of the elder young gentlemen. And the tribute to the mistress speaks. I wish sometimes that their hearts would turn to their father. His is open to them, if they knew. But if they did, he would do something to repel them; he is driven by something within. He is master of everyone in the house but himself."

"I am tired of talking about him," said Halliday.

"Then we will drop the subject," said Ainger, in a pleasant tone.

"I will resume it," said Mrs. Frost. "Is he ashamed of what he has done?"

Ainger smiled to himself.

"Does silence mean consent?" said Kate.

"It does not," said Ainger. "The opposite is implied."

"What has he to be proud of?" said Halliday.

"I don't know, Halliday. It does not seem to me that he has anything."

"He is not proud of this business?"

"I would not say he is not. I said he was in some respects a child."

"It must have taken courage," said Kate.

"Courage or cowardice?" said Ainger, lifting his brows. "It must be a moot point."

"It may be both," said Kate.

"I call it courage," said Bennet. "I should never dare to do it."

"Then of course you call it courage," said Mrs. Frost. "It is only right."

"There is something in it," said Ainger. "To go alone into the dark! I don't see myself doing it, though I have the courage to face life."

"It is strange that we all have it," said Kate.

"I do admire myself," said Madge.

"Well, we know that," said Halliday.

"The round and task," said Ainger. "There may be more in them than we know."

"There is not any more," said Mrs. Frost.

"Ah, that is where the courage may lie."

"What next?" said Halliday. "You will soon think it needs courage to sit down to your meals."

"Well, who shall say?" said Ainger.

"I will," said Mrs. Frost. "It needs none."

"I do not know," said Ainger. "Meals may be a crucial point. I am often glad I do not sit down to those in the dining-room. It is enough to be a witness of them."

"It may be well to see how matters lie," said Kate.

"Essential is the word, Kate. It helps me to deal with them afterwards. Breakfast is often the key to my day."

"And to theirs too, I suppose," said Madge.

"To theirs too, Madge. We need not pursue the point. But I watch the signs with an anxious eye. I often stand behind that table with my heart standing still and my blood running cold."

"And does Simon do the same?" said Bennet.

"He may speak for himself," said Ainger.

"No," said Simon. "They usually seem to be polite."

"Polite!" said Ainger. "I prefer any other sign. If there is any sort of outlet, the air may be clear. I know what my day is going to be, by the time I carry out those trays."

"How did you feel when you thought the master might die?" said Madge.

"I will express it in a word, Madge. It is a good thing the suspense was short."

"I wonder if he is glad or sorry to be well again."

"Sorry, if he knows his own mind," said Halliday.

"I should not wish him to do that," said Ainger. "It would be to wish him not himself. I must try to give him hope."

"It is a pity you did not do that before."

"I have said that I blame myself."

"So you are not to blame any longer," said Mrs. Frost.

"People tend to the view," said Kate.

"Then there are exceptions to the rule," said Ainger, in a quiet tone.

"Are the signs of low spirits easy to read?" said Kate.

"Signs were wanting," said Ainger, in a deeper tone. "He contrived not to give them. It is a point I do not miss. It shows the scope of the resolve."

"He must be in a shamefaced mood."

"No," said Ainger, shaking his head with a smile, "he is lying on the sofa as if he were suffering from convalescence. And I cannot look at that sofa without a shudder, and the thought of him being carried away from it, white and still. I caught a glimpse of my own face in the glass, and it was the colour of a sheet."

"So you remembered to look at yourself as well as at him," said Halliday.

"It is a providence that I bethought myself to enter the

room," went on Ainger, as if he had not heard. "I pass over the shock to myself. It is a thing to be disposed of."

"Do you think he will do it again?" said Madge.

"I do not. I have his word. I bethought myself to exact it."

"I should think Mr. Clare would keep the tablets away from him," said Bennet.

"He may," said Ainger. "He may scorn to do so."

"When did you see the master?" said Simon.

"I have had free access to him all the time."

"You did not seem to avail yourself of it?" said Halliday.

Ainger looked at him for a moment.

"Halliday, he lay unconscious."

"Were you able to say a word to him, when he was in the shadow?" said Kate.

"I tried to lighten that passage for him, as I hope someone will one day do it for me."

"You talk as if he had died," said Halliday.

"The outcome was veiled in doubt."

"He was in the valley," said Kate.

"How does Mr. Clare take it?" said Bennet.

"As hard as would be expected. We have exchanged a word. But it is a case where feelings lie beyond."

"So you have had the position of general supporter," said Halliday.

"And little as accrues to me from it, I ask no other."

"What was the master's complaint against life?" said Kate.

"Life itself," said Ainger, in a deep tone.

"What does the mistress say to all of it?"

"Nothing as far as I am concerned. We are not on the terms. She maintains her distance, as she has a right. The gentlemen decide to ignore it."

"Does she feel it rebounds on her?" said Kate.

"She has given no sign, nor not to me. It is not her tendency."

"How soon will the master be well?" said Madge.

"He is able to talk to-day," said Bennet. "Mrs. Clare

and his father are with him in the library. The children are to go later."

"He would have something to listen to, if I were in their place," said Halliday.

"Halliday, how your thoughts run on common lines!" said Ainger, seeming to control himself by an effort.

"We can imagine the scene," said Bennet, her tone recognising the limits of this method.

"I could be the first to do so," said Ainger, "and in consequence am the last who wishes to. I feel the recoil."

The scene was in progress at the moment, and was outwardly as was said. Cassius lay on the couch, and his father and his wife stood by him. It was the first occasion when talk could take its normal course.

"Well, we cannot congratulate you on your recovery, my boy. It is the opposite of what you hoped."

"I hope you congratulate yourselves on it," said Cassius, in a weak voice. "For myself, I begin to see that life has its claims."

"Begin to see it! Then you took your time about arranging to get out of it."

"We have to stay where our lot is cast."

"That was not your view," said his wife.

"Ah, Flavia, I am hardly in the mood for that tone to-day. Things were somehow too much for me. I must learn to see them differently."

"They will not be different," said Mr. Clare. "It is a long habit to break."

"Does an attempt to escape from life give you a hold on it?" said Flavia. "It seems a method that might defeat itself."

"Ah, Flavia, you are yourself," said Cassius. "And you do not remember that the same cannot be said of me."

"What was your reason for doing it, Cassius?"

"I felt that life had little to give me, and that no one wanted what I had to give. It seemed to be time for my place to know me no more."

"Did you spare a thought to the rest of us?" said Mr. Clare.

"I did, my dear old father. I can tell you my actual thought. It was that you and I would soon be united, and that no one else had need of me."

"You may have had a grievance," said his wife. "But not great enough to drive you to your death."

"You hardly seem serious, Flavia. Is it not a serious thing?"

"I am trying to find out what it is."

"It is as I have told you. I will not try to estimate it. I may be a person whose hold on life is light."

"There is something about it I do not understand. I have no choice but to pursue it."

"No choice but to harass and harry me?" said Cassius, gently.

"None but to try and discover your reason for what you did."

"To be without heart and hope is reason enough."

"Not for many of us, and not for you. I am not a stranger to you."

"My poor wife, that is just what you are. It is what you have always been. How clearly I see it! It did not make me less alone."

"What was in your mind? Or what was on it? I ask you to tell me the truth."

"I am not the hero of a detective story, Flavia."

"You need not be so longer than you like," said Mr. Clare.

"You cannot face the truth," said Cassius, looking at his wife. "You know it and will not accept it. There is no more to be said."

"More will be said and more will be thought. You are right that I do not accept your account as the true one."

"Do you accept it, Father? Do you take my word?"

"I do not expect you to tell us what you are keeping to yourself, my boy. What is the truth about one thing? Are you glad you failed to do your work?"

"I may get to be glad," said Cassius, wearily. "This is not the way to make me so. I did not expect these dealings. I was not prepared for an attack. I see it is easier to face death than to face life."

"Well, life presents many problems, and death none. But it has not been your way to be overset by them."

"You do not know how I have met them."

"I know as much about you as you do yourself, my boy."

"It is as true of you as it can be of anyone. But we go by ourselves through life. If anyone has saved me from it, it is you."

"There will be other people in the next world, if your theories are true," said Flavia.

"They will have cast off their mortal guise, and with them their mortal qualities."

"I should not relinquish my resolve to pursue the truth about this."

"I suppose you cannot imagine hopelessness?"

"I think I can, though I have not experienced it. But have you done either, Cassius?"

"So you know me no better than that, after nine years?"

"After that time I know you as well as that."

"After fifty-two years I do the same," said Mr. Clare.

"We are unfamiliar with this new guise," said Flavia.

"Perhaps the other was a guise," said Cassius. "Perhaps you are seeing my real self for the first time."

"No, no," said his father, "the other would have become real by now. And what reason had you to hide yourself? You saw none."

"Well, this is leading us nowhere."

"That is the fault we find with it," said Flavia. "But it will lead us somewhere in the end."

"I cannot help you any more."

"It may be true, my boy," said Mr. Clare. "You are not able to bring yourself to it. And you would have a right to keep your own counsel, if your actions affected no one else."

"There is no mystery," said Cassius.

"That is the word," said his father.

"Well, have it as you will. There is some dark secret."

"Those words will do as well."

"The secret may not be so dark," said Flavia. "Things become so when kept in darkness."

Cassius compared his watch with the clock on the chimney-piece and glanced at the door. Sounds were heard outside.

"Did you arrange for the children to come?" said his wife.

"Yes," said Cassius, looking again at the watch, as if to check their exactitude.

"So that your interview with us should not be too long?"

"I knew how much I could stand," said Cassius, simply. "Well, so you have all come to see your father. You know he has been ill?"

"No, Toby has," said the latter.

"He was upset this morning," said Megan.

"Poor little boy!" said Toby, looking at his father.

"Yes, poor little Toby! But Father has been worse than that."

"No, Father better now."

"Toby can run about," said Cassius, "and Father has to lie on the sofa."

Toby laid his head down on this support, and watched his father out of the corner of his eye for a model of invalid deportment.

"Quite well now," he said, looking up. "Father and Toby."

"No, Father will not be well yet."

Toby resignedly replaced his head.

"What is the name of your illness?" said Henry to Cassius.

"It is something you would not understand."

"But it must have a name. The doctor must have called it something."

"I think it would now be called general weakness and depression."

"But what was it at first?"

"Why do you want to know? The name does not make much difference."

"I want to tell people about it, when they say it was not an illness."

"What do they say it was?"

"That does not matter, if I can tell them the name. The weakness was just the ending of it."

"The after effects," said Megan.

"Poor Father very sad," said Toby, without raising his head. "Very sad and want to die. But wake up again."

"Do people say that?" said Cassius.

"We heard them saying things," said Megan. "They didn't mean us to hear. And we didn't know they would say them."

"But you knew no better than to listen?"

"We were not listening," said Henry. "Megan told you that we heard. But I daresay we might have listened. There isn't anyone who wouldn't have, when it was a thing like that."

"Why were you as sad as that?" said Megan.

"I can hardly tell you the reasons. I hope you will never be so sad."

"Everyone is sad sometimes," said Henry. "But they don't do what you did. Will you be put in prison?"

"No, of course I shall not."

"I thought that to kill yourself was against the law."

"There is no need to use such words. This was not much more than a mistake."

"Do you mean you did it by accident?"

"Well, I hardly knew what I was doing."

"Then perhaps it would not count. Perhaps you were delirious. People didn't know it was like that. They thought you meant to do it."

"If I had done a good action, no one would have heard of it," said Cassius, looking round.

"They would certainly have had less opportunity," said Mr. Clare. "It would have made less talk."

"Have you ever done one?" said Henry. "You know I don't mean you haven't. I just wanted to know."

"I suppose so from time to time. Have you?"

"Well, I don't think so. I can't think of one."

"Well, I declare, neither can I," said Cassius, half-laughing. "I declare that I can't. But I suppose I can hardly have gone through life without doing something for somebody."

"People generally count supporting their children," said Megan.

"Well, I do not. That does not put me apart from other men."

"And your good action must do that?" said Mr. Clare. "You would kill two birds with one stone."

The elder boys had entered the room, and Fabian came up to his father.

"We have been fortunate, Father," he said, holding out his hand. "I am so thankful, and so is everyone. We could not have spared you."

Cassius took the hand and sent his eyes over his son's face. Guy came and stood by his brother.

"You said you had never done a good action," he said, in a hurried, even tone. "But you let Mother come and see us, and changed things for us all. And you let her go on coming. It does put you apart from other men."

"Did your mother tell you to say these things?"

"She did not tell us what to say," said Fabian.

"Then I congratulate you in my turn. You have done well. You may tell you mother that from me."

There was a long silence.

"You did not tell your son to make a speech?" said Cassius to Flavia.

"No, I leave him to depend on himself."

141

"What he said was certainly different."

"Which kind of approach do you prefer?"

"You made a beautiful speech, my boy," said Cassius, suddenly to Guy. "You brought comfort to your father when he needed it. You have made him proud of you, and so has your brother. I am a happier man, and I had need of happiness."

Toby ran up and stood ready to share in the compliments.

"And Toby is a comfort to Father by being himself."

"And Henry and Megan," said Toby, with an embracing gesture. "And Bennet and Eliza and Mother."

"What would have happened to us, if you had died?" said Henry. "This house would have belonged to Fabian; so we should still have had a home. But would other things have been different?"

"And Ainger and William," added Toby.

"Would you not have found that losing me made a difference?" said Cassius, looking at his son.

"Yes, but I knew about that."

"So that is how you talked, when you thought I might be going to die."

"Well, we couldn't have helped it, if you had," said Megan. "We shouldn't have had to feel ashamed about it. That is unfair when people haven't done anything. And when a thing is done on purpose, it isn't even sad."

"It is sad that anyone should want to do such a thing."

"Not if he wanted to when he had an ordinary life. If he had had pain or sorrow, it would be different."

"Life itself can be a sorrow, my child."

"Only because of what is in it. We are supposed to like life itself. Will you be happier now you have done this? Your life won't be any different."

"I shall be more resigned. And I hope my life will be a little different. I hope something will come out of it, that will make it so. And I must remember what you say, and try to like life itself."

"Toby said it," said Toby, coming up with something in his hands.

"What have you there?" said Cassius.

Toby displayed a box containing various objects.

"Where did you get that box?"

"Open drawer," said his son.

"Go and put it back again and shut the drawer."

"No," said Toby.

"Do as Father tells you at once."

"Bottle," said Toby, making a selection from the box.

"He will break it," said Megan.

"Oh, no," said Toby, his voice quavering into mirth. "Only hold it. When it break, can't help it, poor little boy."

Cassius reached towards the bottle, but desisted and drummed his fingers on the couch.

"Give the bottle to me," said Mr. Clare. "It is mine, and I have my use for it."

"Rattle it," said his grandson.

"No, it is almost empty. It will not make any noise."

Toby showed that this was not the case, and his grandfather stood with his eyes on it. A change seemed to come into the room. It seemed that time was standing still. Mr. Clare and Flavia met each other's eyes, and the former took the bottle and emptied it on his hand.

"Seven tablets! And there were eleven there. So you took four, my son."

His unusual ending gave weight to his words.

"Yes, I took four," said Cassius, going into deliberate mirth. "Enough to make me unconscious and to do no more. But it did a good deal more. It has done its work. And I should not like to face it again, I can tell you. I began to think I should breathe my last. I almost had the experience I was supposed to have had. I thought my last hour had come. But I played a proper trick on all of you. The weak point was that I played it on myself as well. You need not think I did not suffer for what I did, if that is any comfort to you. If four tablets did that, ten would indeed have done the whole."

"Well, we knew that," said his father.

"And if you all say it served me right, I say the same to you," said Cassius, his tones swelling. "You deserved to think you had driven me to my death, when you had done all you could to empty my life. It was the right and fair return; it was poetic justice. So I don't want any solemn faces or speaking silences or exchange of glances. Things are fair and square between us, and there is an end of it."

"There is also a beginning," said Flavia. "Another conception of you, a mistrust of what you say and do, a question of your presentation of yourself. A difference that will go through our lives and die with us."

"And have you had so much trust in me? There has been little sign of it. We cannot lose what we have never had. I have not to face much there."

"Did Father pretend he had taken more pills than he had?" said Megan.

"He did, my child. That is what he pretended," said Cassius, going into further mirth. "And he does not regret it. And he hopes you will never be driven to a like course, and that if you are, you will achieve more by it."

"I don't understand why you did it, or what you wanted to achieve."

"Neither do I," said Henry.

"Neither do I," said Flavia.

"No," said Cassius, looking at them. "You would not understand. The heart can only know itself."

"You let me know some of it, my boy," said Mr. Clare.

"I did, my dear old father. And what I should have done without your listening ear I do not know."

"You could hardly have done more than you have."

"I could have done the whole thing."

"No, you could not, being as you are. We can only act according to ourselves."

"I really thought of it."

"We are not talking of thoughts. They cover a wide ground."

"You are a strange man, Cassius," said Flavia. "I see I have not known you."

"And you are a strange woman. And I have always known you. And now I know you better."

"You have put yourself in a class apart."

"No, I have not. I have put myself in the class of weak, erring mortals to which we all belong, to which you belong yourself. I am not removed from you by a single act. What about you, who drove me to it? What should be said of that? No, you are not to go, children. I refuse to be left alone with this woman. Father does not want to be left alone with Mater." Cassius changed his tone and put his hand on Toby's head. "She is vexed with him and makes him afraid of her. Toby must stay and take care of him."

Toby placed himself in front of his father and looked round in challenge, and Flavia glanced at him and looked away.

"I think Mother is in the hall," said Fabian. "She was coming to see us to-day. May we go out to her, Father?"

"You must ask Mater that," said Mr. Clare.

"Mater always lets us see her."

"Ask her in; ask her in," said Cassius. "We have nothing to hide. She may as well hear what she must hear in the end, and hear the truth instead of some distortion of it. Let her swell the chorus of my judges. Come in, Catherine, and join them in their verdict on me. I know you and Flavia have but one thought between you."

"They do not need more than one for this matter," said Mr. Clare.

"Well, Catherine, what have you heard of me? You need not be afraid to say. I am not used to being spared."

There was a pause.

"I heard that you found things too much. I heard that you tried to end them."

"Well, well, it was not quite that," said Cassius, with

another sound of mirth and his eyes turned aside. "I hardly know how to tell you. I have put myself in an awkward place. You may think in almost a ridiculous one; I can understand that view. Or rather it is chance that has done it; I thought things out myself. Ask Flavia to tell you. You would rather hear it from her. And she can put things in a word better than I can."

"No, it is your own history, my boy," said Mr. Clare. "No one else can tell it from the first."

"Well, then, I did not take the full dose," said Cassius, looking in front of him and speaking easily. "Only enough to make me unconscious and do no more. I thought of taking it, and then the will to live, or the impulse of life, or whatever it was, checked me and led me to a compromise. Compromise; yes, that is the word. And I carried it through. I did not fail in my purpose. I hoodwinked my father and my wife. And they are not easy people to deceive; you must have found that. I mean you would understand it. They accepted the whole thing. And upon my word I was near to accepting it myself. It was a dire experience, recovering from that trance. I find myself feeling I have had a narrow escape. I find myself in a mood of thankfulness. It shows how near I was to the actual thing."

"It surely shows your distance from it," said Flavia.

"Well, you ought to be glad of that. It ought to be a relief to you. You don't seem to have taken any lesson from what I have done."

"But you seem to have taken one yourself," said Mr. Clare. "And it is you who needed it."

"And you have not done it, Cassius," said Flavia. "We cannot go so far from the facts."

"Did you confess the truth?" said Catherine to Cassius, in a tone that seemed to come from their life together.

"Go on with your tale, my boy," said Mr. Clare. "It is no one else's."

"Well, no, I did not," said Cassius, with a little laugh. "I meant to carry the matter through and let the deception do its work. And I hope in a measure it has done it. But Toby found the bottle with the tablets that were left, and the number told their tale and exposed his father."

"You put it well, my boy," said Mr. Clare.

"Yes, well, I can put things into words when I like," said his son, in a modest tone. "I can express myself when there is need. I seem to be able to. I don't know if it is true of everyone."

"No one must talk of this outside the house," said Flavia.

"No, it would swell to all kinds of proportions," said Cassius, as if not averse to the idea. "I should be said to have put an end to myself ten times over."

"You would be said to have tried to do so once," said Mr. Clare. "No doubt you will be. And it is at once better and worse than the truth."

"The subject will be rife in the place for the next weeks," said his son. "Then it will die away. One cannot expect to be a hero—to be on people's tongues for ever. It will remain with me, as our moments of danger do remain. And it was a moment of danger, Flavia, however much you look at me. You will never know how near I was to the end."

"It is you who seem not to know," said his father.

"We have all been near to things that are beyond us," said Flavia, "in the sense that we imagine ourselves doing them, without any intention of it. And it is not very near. We have all stood on the edge of a cliff and pictured ourselves going over."

"I stood on the edge," said Cassius.

"Poor Father!" said Toby, pausing to look at him.

"Yes, poor Father! No one seems to know how poor he is. There are unkind faces on every side. Well, Fabian, you are wearing a dark expression. What do you think of what has happened?"

"I can't help being surprised, Father."

"And shocked?" said Cassius.

"Well, yes, I suppose I am."

"By what you thought had happened, or by what has?"

"It is a different kind of feeling. I think more by the pretence."

"So you are as straight as a die, are you? You could never leave the narrow path. And Guy is of the same mind. He could not be anything else."

"I could, but I do think the same about this."

"And what does Megan think? She has a mind of her own."

"Well, it was not very honest. I think everyone's mind would be the same."

"Oh, you are a set of little, literal creatures! Would you rather be without a father than have one who had made a mistake?"

"No, but we would rather have the usual kind of father."

"It wasn't a mistake," said Henry. "It was meant to be a lasting deceit."

"Deception," said Cassius, easily. "So you are equally disturbed. You think I acted a lie?"

"Well, I can't help seeing you did. And you would be angry if we did it."

"I don't think there has been much wrong with our training," said Cassius, smiling at Flavia, as though the situation were an easy one. "But I don't think I was so cold and conventional when I was a child."

"So you are the perfect example," said Mr. Clare.

"There are better things than perfection, my dear old father. Things that have their place in the imperfection of human life. The things that I would have chosen to have, that I shall miss until I go to my grave."

Guy and Megan looked at their father with compassion.

"My little son and daughter!" said Cassius, holding out his arms. "Father knows what you feel. You have sound hearts beneath the surface they have imposed on you. Father understands."

Fabian and Henry regarded the scene in resignation, and Toby came up and surveyed it.

"Come, my boy, you have made enough trouble," said Mr. Clare.

"My little ones," went on Cassius, his arms still open. "I admit this is a comfort to me. I am glad to see tears in my children's eyes for their father."

"I would rather see something other than tears," said Flavia.

"Well, I would not, when tears are the right thing, the proper tribute to other people and to them. If these are a tribute to me, I take it as such and welcome it. It shows them at their best, and shows me what they are. Why, Ainger, I did not see you. Have you been moving about in the room all the time?"

Ainger gave a faint start, as if he had been doing this in solitude.

"So you have been a witness of a family scene. Well, it is not the first time."

"I beg your pardon, sir?" said Ainger, pausing as if interrupted.

"It would be no good to keep anything from you. But it need not go through the house."

"That is not the destination of what is reposed in me, sir. But would not the truth be better than what has passed for it?"

"Oh, you have been here as long as that, have you?"

Ainger flicked a duster over a table and looked with a faint frown at the result.

"You mean that the pretence I made is better than a real attempt at the same thing."

"It is of an easier nature, sir."

"Yes, I suppose it is. People don't seem to take to the idea of not seeing me in my place. I suppose I have filled it in my own way. I don't know what made me do such a thing. I hardly know what word to use."

"It was impetuous, sir," said Ainger, not himself at a loss.

"Yes, I lost my head as anyone might, and the drug was

149

there. Do as you will about making it known. You may use your own judgement."

"I have already used it as I have implied, sir," said Ainger, putting cigars at his master's hand before leaving the room with a smothered eagerness.

"Dear Ainger!" said Toby, looking after him.

"He is a good friend," said Cassius.

"You make too much of a friend of him," said Flavia.

"Too much of a friend?" said her husband, with lifted brows. "How can I have too much of such a thing? I have little enough in my life."

"There is nothing he does not know."

"And too much that he may know, Flavia?" said Cassius, just smiling at her and shaking his head. "Ah, we both have things we are not proud of. It is not all on my side."

"It is a mistake to ignore conventions. There is always a reason behind them."

"I have never been bound by such things."

"But it is a pity to be blind to them."

"Blind?" said Cassius, leaning back and looking before him. "Ah, there is too much blindness in the world, too much in this house, and to deeper things than conventions."

Ainger recollected himself at the kitchen door and entered with his hand on his chin and his eyes down.

"Well, is there anything to tell?" said Madge, interpreting the signs.

Ainger just glanced at her and did not move his hand.

"Well, what is it, Mr. Ainger?" said Kate.

Ainger spared another glance.

"Put it into plain words," said Halliday.

"I will do so, if I resort to words."

"And what is there against that?"

"I am weighing the reasons," said Ainger, and continued to do so.

"Are you at liberty to make the disclosure?" said Kate.

"If I were not, should I be debating the point? It would be foregone."

"You can feel the matter is in your hands?"

"It has been put into them, Kate."

"By the master?"

"Now, Kate, with whom else am I on that footing?" said Ainger, with a smile.

"And did the mistress support it?"

"If silence indicates consent."

"It often does not," said Mrs. Frost.

"No, Mrs. Frost, that is true," said Ainger. "And looking back, I am not sure that it did. That is why I debate the matter. I do not render less, because less is given. I do not see myself in that light."

"You can hold your tongue if you want to," said Halliday.

Ainger looked at him and just inclined his head.

"There is no need for you all to sit in silence," he said, presently.

"Everything is not to be referred to yourself," said Halliday.

"This is," said Madge. "It is the hush of suspense. Suppose he does not tell us!"

"There is no need to suppose it."

"None at all," said Ainger, cordially. "You need not meet trouble half-way."

"Trouble is too much of a word," said Halliday. "It is a trifling thing."

"Not to me," said Ainger. "It concerns those near to me and above me, a twofold claim."

"Is the truth in any way derogatory?" said Kate.

"Not to my mind, Kate, with my knowledge. It rather moves a pitying smile."

"So it does," said Mrs. Frost, with her eyes on his face.

"Yes, Mrs. Frost, I do not suppress it," said Ainger, illustrating the words. "It is the attitude that meets the case."

"So it is the master himself," said Kate.

"Well, what else is there in Ainger's horizon?" said Halliday.

"It is the chief thing, Halliday. I endorse it. He is the figure."

"Is it anything to do with his action?" said Kate.

"It throws light on it," said Ainger.

"Wasn't it what was thought?"

"It was and it was not. That expresses it."

"Did someone else give him the tablets?" said Madge.

"That is not a line to pursue in this house. It refutes itself."

"Did he fail to judge the amount?" said Kate.

"I may say that he used his judgement, Kate."

"Did he take too little on purpose?" said Mrs. Frost.

Ainger inclined his head.

"You have said it, Mrs. Frost. He took what brought oblivion and gave the impression."

"What was that?" said Madge.

"That he wished to terminate his span on earth," said Ainger, lowering his tone and his eyes.

"What was his reason?" said Kate.

"There were reasons when you were near to him. They remain in their place."

"How did the truth come to light?"

"The usual trivial thing. In this case the number of tablets remaining. They were found by one of the children."

"And we are to waste our pity!" said Halliday. "I give it to other people and give him something else. A sorry course."

"The essence of sadness and helplessness, Halliday. The man of calibre at bay! It moves the heart like a child's trouble."

"Well, he is your child. Or was it your younger brother? When I have seen him, he has been something else."

"You are right that it is complex, Halliday."

"What does the mistress feel on the occasion?" said Kate.

"She takes the view to be expected, but violates nothing. And Mr. Clare applied his touch in his own way."

"So the master had to appear in a sorry light."

"Strange to say, Kate, he did not do so. It was because

he did not feel it. Nothing else was needed to prove him himself."

"Why did they want you all that time?" said Halliday. "What could you do for them?"

"They did not want me so much as assume my presence. I found it was taken for granted. And I could do nothing for them, Halliday. It was not the occasion. But something passed between us. I felt it going from me to them. My presence was not superfluous."

"You were a long time outside the door," said Simon.

"And where were you?" said Ainger, turning on him.

"I came to see if I could help. But you were not doing anything."

"You are wrong. I was doing my duty, odd though that may seem to you."

"It may seem odd to him," said Mrs. Frost.

"Well, it will be a long time before his duty lies along that line."

"Mine has not done so yet," said Mrs. Frost.

"It might be said of all of us," said Kate. "But there are circumstances."

"The master will approve," said Ainger, on a satisfied note, "when I make use of easy reference. Indeed it has come to pass. It spares him words; it saves the shame-faced touch, and that I could not bear for him."

"You are birds of a feather," said Halliday.

"Well, closeness tends to resemblance. I have heard it said. But when the gulf narrows, I establish it. The master may be trusted to me. I hold his position dearer than he does himself."

"Does Mr. Clare know of your methods?" said Madge.

"Ah, there is not much that escapes the old gentleman. He and I have exchanged a look on the occasion. It would not be complete without one."

The bell rang, and Ainger sped from the room with a startled look, as though fearing the meaning of the summons.

CHAPTER XII

"Will you have some more coffee, Cassius?" said Flavia.
Her husband made no reply.

"Will you have some more coffee?"

Cassius indicated the full cup at his elbow and looked before him.

"What do you see that we do not?" said Mr. Clare.

His son turned his eyes on him.

"We see what we see," he said in a moment. "Some of us nothing; some of us more; some of us much."

"And to which class do you belong?"

Cassius turned on his father a smile of some kindness.

"To which do you? We all see ourselves in some way."

"Only one class would be needed," said Flavia. "We should all choose the same. If this talk has anything in it."

Cassius transferred the smile to her, and kept it on her for a moment. If the talk had not anything in it, the smile had. It carried tolerance, amusement, perception.

Ainger bent towards his master's plate in concerned enquiry.

"I have not touched that," said the latter, in an incidental tone. "It need not be wasted."

"No, sir," said Ainger, in neutral acceptance of this thrift, as he removed the plate.

"Are you not having anything to eat, Cassius?" said Flavia.

"You can see I am not. I saw you notice it some time ago. It was not worth your while to speak of it."

"That would have ensured your having nothing."

"It has been proved, my boy," said Mr. Clare.

Cassius vaguely drummed his hands on the table.

"Would you like some fresh toast?" said his wife.

Her husband turned his head from side to side.

"What are you doing to-day?"

"Doing?" said Cassius, with a faint frown. "How do you mean? In what way am I making myself useful?"

"In what way are you to pass your time?"

"Time passes of itself," said Cassius, in a deeper tone. "It does not need our dealings with it."

"But it has them," said his father. "We use it for all we do. How are you using it to-day? That is your wife's meaning."

"Bailiff; tenants; gardener," said Cassius, just enunciating the words.

"And they are wearing you out?"

"I suppose they do their part towards it day by day."

"If I may interpolate, sir," said Ainger, "they may not be available this morning. The flower show in the village will engross their attention."

"They will come to me if I want them."

"Yes, certainly, sir."

"It is not a public holiday."

"It has come to be observed as a local one, sir."

"Do you want to go gallivanting with the rest?"

"I am familiar with our exhibits, sir. If the others are inferior, why see them? And if superior, we may want to see them even less."

"Ours are hardly up to standard this year."

"For a reason that need not be discussed, sir," said Ainger, as if this would be a needless breach of convention.

"The want of another gardener? We cannot afford a second. We might perhaps have a boy."

"I doubt if William has the tolerance, sir."

"Do you find that yours is taxed?"

"Well, I am inured, sir."

"And William will become so, if I wish it."

"We cannot add a cubit to our stature, sir."

"There are several boys without work in the village."

"We do not want Master Toby among them, sir," said Ainger, with a smile.

"So your hours will be empty to-day?" said Mr. Clare to his son.

The latter just glanced at him and leaned his head on his hand.

"Accounts," he said, in a just audible tone.

"The library will be ready, sir," said Ainger.

"I have said it is always to be so."

"The desk and the writing materials were my reference, sir."

"And the ledgers and rent accounts," said Cassius, still supporting his head. "I shall want them at my hand."

"That is their situation, sir."

"How are you passing your time, Flavia?" said Cassius.

"I shall be doing the usual things."

"And is that an answer?"

"Housekeeping, letters, gardening," said Flavia, putting her own head on her hand and echoing his tone.

"Smoking, newspapers, dozing," said Mr. Clare, more lightly.

Cassius appeared not to see or hear.

"Wine-cellar, silver, sideboard, sir," said Ainger, in a tone of coming to his master's aid. "Arrears accumulate as soon as effort fluctuates."

"How about the wine from London?" said Cassius.

"It is still in London, as far as I am informed, sir."

"When did you write for it, Cassius?" said Flavia.

"I cannot be sure of the exact day."

"Did you write at all?" said his father. "It is a thing that would be hard for you."

"Then it would be natural if I did not write."

"And it is natural that the wine has not come," said his wife.

"Can I indite the order for you, sir?" said Ainger.

"Well, you may copy the rough draft on my desk, if I have omitted to do so."

"The one I dictated, sir? I do not need to recapitulate. My memory is one of my characteristics."

"You have not been active in the matter, my boy," said Mr. Clare.

Cassius leaned back in his chair, active in nothing.

"Are you not yourself to-day? Or are you too much so?"

"We are all too much ourselves at breakfast," said Cassius, looking round the table to encounter proof of this. "I don't think there are exceptions."

"No, no, you are a person apart."

"I have felt that for a long time."

"We all have to get used to it," said Flavia, "and it has its own comfort."

"We live at such different levels," said her husband.

"But always at a deep one ourselves. When someone else is bereaved, we always say how easily he has got over it."

"I think of my mother every day," said Cassius; "my dear mother whose sympathy flowed from her. Perhaps she taught me to expect too much."

"She did so," said Mr. Clare, "and you learned it from her. A woman with one son may serve him in that way. It was a simple case."

"I don't know why you want so much sympathy," said Flavia.

"No?" said Cassius, resting his eyes on her.

"You are not an unfortunate man."

"No?"

"Upon my word I don't know what the trouble is," said Mr. Clare.

"There is no trouble," said Flavia, "and we should not make one. There are enough and to spare."

"A truism," said her husband.

"They are generally true."

"They sometimes have a modicum of truth. I suppose that is what you mean."

"No, I meant what I said. That is what you mean yourself."

"I have never had to make troubles," said Cassius. "My share has come to me."

"So you have been spared the pains," said his father. "And I do not know why you should take them."

"I have had rather trials than troubles," said Flavia.

"You must be glad of that," said Cassius, in a cordial tone. "And we are glad for you."

"Trials have a way of being more continuous. They are more involved in ordinary life. They stand less by themselves."

"They are woven into life," said Cassius, dreamily, "a part of its warp and woof. You would not be prepared for that. We must not look for experience from those who have not had it."

"Is mine any good to you this morning?" said his father. "I have had enough, and it is at your service."

"I shall be glad to be with you when my work is done. Flavia has her companionship."

"What do you know about my plans for the day?" said his wife.

"Know about them?" said Cassius, looking up with a faint frown. "There is nothing to know, is there? They are stereotyped."

"And in what way?"

"Well, either you will go to your friend or she will come to you. Is there any alternative?"

"Are you speaking of the boys' mother?"

"Flavia, that is going too far," said Cassius, almost laughing.

"There are other people in my life."

Her husband raised his brows.

"You forget that I have children myself."

"I may sometimes do so, now that there is less to remind me of it, now you are focused on one point."

"You know less about me than you think."

Cassius sent his eyes over her and did not endorse this.

"I do not claim to know everything about you."

"Well, no, I suppose not," said Cassius, with a faint sound of amusement.

"And I should have thought you were the easier to judge."

Cassius laughed outright.

"People talk of our seeing ourselves as others see us," said Mr. Clare. "It is the way we ourselves do so, that should concern them."

"Especially when we make it clear," said Cassius, looking at his wife with another tremble of mirth.

"This is not sincere talk," she said.

"Is it not?" said her husband. "It is honest of you to admit it."

"You are a sophist, my boy," said Mr. Clare.

"Well, is breakfast at an end?" said Cassius, rising from the table, and seeming to chance to push his full cup into view. "If so, I will go to the library."

"Breakfast has not begun for Cassius," said Flavia, as the door closed. "But what are we to do?"

"Nothing, my dear. Nothing can be done. We are helpless in the matter."

"I wonder how much he suffers in these moods."

"We can only know what we do. We can learn no more."

"I always feel I ought to be able to prevent them."

"I have felt the same. But we rank ourselves too high. We cannot be of use."

"What Cassius needs is a perfect wife. I see what it would do for him. But perfection might do a good deal for many of us. It may be too simple a view."

"It is not only the complex that is true. We all need perfection in other people, and might be the better for it."

"I attempted the impossible in marrying him. Or do I mean something beyond me?"

"You may mean them both. Cassius stands as what he is. He offers no revised version of himself."

Cassius had gone to the library, sat down at the desk and rested his head on his hands. Once or twice he raised it and drew some papers towards him, but soon relinquished them. Ainger entered, laid the list of wine before him, and withdrew in one swift movement. Cassius looked up at him as he reached the door.

"So it is thought that wine matters, Ainger. What is your feeling about it?"

"Well, sir, in our ordinary life ordinary things have their niche."

"I somehow feel I am no longer living it. There has come a change for me of late. I hardly know how to express it."

"I should suggest you have not been yourself since your illness, sir."

"That is a kind way of putting it, Ainger. It holds a kind thought. Everyone's thought of me is not so kind. I have to get used to hostile eyes."

"Would it not be truer to say 'disapproving', sir? There is no hostility in any glance I have seen cast upon you."

"Disapproval is a cheerless companion. It throws a cold shadow on one's path. I may have invited it, but it dogs my steps. I ask myself if I shall always be followed by it."

"Not if you give it time and make no more place for it, sir."

"Ah, you too think the less of me."

"I think the more about you, sir, and with no less feeling," said Ainger, as he went to the door.

Cassius looked at the list of wine as if he did not follow it, took up an envelope and put the two together, but seemed unable to connect them, and remained with them in his hands.

An hour or two later Ainger came to Mr. Clare.

"We are in trouble again, sir. I hesitate to tell you. I hardly like to employ the words."

"Well, make up your mind. Either use them or tell someone else to do so."

"The master again, sir. He is lying on the sofa, as before. And it is not two hours since we exchanged a word. What course are we to follow? Making much of it defeats its purpose."

"I will come with you and see him."

"It is what I hoped you would suggest, sir."

The two men went to the library and Mr. Clare stood by his son.

"Yes, the same thing again. A second time. I suppose breakfast was leading up to it. I see now that it was."

"It did strike a warning note, sir. But we could not forecast this. We have had breakfasts of that kind before."

"What is our life to be, if we are to fear it? We cannot live under the threat. It would be not to live at all."

"If you will be advised, sir, you will do nothing. Notice feeds the desire for prominence and has the outcome. Neglect is sometimes wholesome. Our seeming to become inured may prevent recurrence. It would have to be done without reward, if you understand me."

"It seems little reward in itself," said Mr. Clare, looking at his son. "Well, he recovered by himself before; the doctor did nothing. We may leave it to happen as it did then, as no doubt he relied on its doing. And we will not have the after-scenes. That was our mistake."

"Yes, sir, we crowned it with success, as it were. Were the tablets where he would come on them?"

"There are some in the desk. I keep them for myself, and must do so. I did not turn the key on them. Why should I do such a thing? He is a man of fifty and my son. And I felt he had done this once and for all. I thought there were signs of it. And there were signs. I know him."

"I should have said the same of myself, sir. It seems we are not to know each other."

"I know my son. I have foretold his actions. I have seen them in his words. I did not foretell this. Can there be a change?"

"I should have thought not, sir. I should have said there

was something immutable. I hope this is not part of it," said Ainger, ending almost with a smile.

"We must see that it is not. We must protect him from himself, and ourselves from him. But it serves no purpose to stand with our eyes on him. He looks as he did last time, and for a while must do so. Last time! What a way to have to talk!"

Mr. Clare turned with a silent step, as if his son were asleep.

"Let me lead you away, sir," said Ainger, putting his hand under his arm. "I will look in on the master myself. Though he does not know it, my eye will be on him. It will not be the first time."

"Come to me, if there is any change. And when your mistress returns, bring her to me."

"I will break it to her myself, sir. I can spare you that. And you may rely on the method. It is fortunate that she is to be away for some hours. When he returns, the worst will be over."

"And the rest will begin. And we have had enough. I do not see why a woman should bear anything, or an old man either. He will not teach me to forget that I am his father, but I can only answer for myself."

"We all have to make our sacrifice for the master, sir. And it seems to bind us together. In a way it is the meaning of the house."

When Flavia returned late in the day, Ainger was waiting in the hall.

"I am both glad and sorry to see you, ma'am. I hope we have done right. We have had our trouble again, and have had to use our own judgement. It could not have been foreseen."

"What is the matter?"

"It is the same thing again, ma'am. The master was found as before. I happened to look in on him. It is a good thing the instinct prompted me. I don't know if the coming event cast its shadow before."

"There was some kind of shadow. It has followed me all day. I ought to have stayed at home. What is the truth?"

"Simply the same as previously, ma'am. Or I trust we can say it is. We thought it best to leave him, as the doctor found nothing to do. But as the hours passed and there was no change, I took it upon myself to send for him. He should be here at any moment. I did not tell Mr. Clare for fear of alarming him. Yes, ma'am, on the sofa, as before."

Flavia was standing by Cassius, as his father had stood. She turned to Ainger at once.

"You are not right that there has been no change. There have been more than one. When did the last one come?"

"I admit I am alarmed myself, ma'am."

"It is useless for me to say that the doctor should have come at once."

"It may partake of wisdom after the event, ma'am."

"It is wisdom nevertheless," said Flavia, turning again to her husband.

The minutes passed in silence. There was nothing to do but live through them. Ainger waited at the door for the doctor, and they hastened to the library. Mr. Clare entered with them, summoned by the sounds.

The silence held and grew. The doctor bent over Cassius. Ainger moved to his hand, obeyed his hurrried word. Some necessary things were done, and he turned and faced the wife and father.

"It is worse this time," said Mr. Clare. "Has he taken more than before?"

"He has taken nothing. This is a different thing. It is a sudden illness. It is an affection of the heart not unusual in middle-aged men. If stimulants had been given in time, it might have been different. I can say it would have been. I should have been sent for at once, as, if you had known, you would have sent for me."

"But how could we know? How could we suspect this second thing? It had all the appearance of the first."

"You could not know. You are not to blame. You thought and did what was natural."

"And now is there any hope?"

The doctor did not answer, and Mr. Clare turned to his son.

"Poor boy, poor boy!" he said.

"Can nothing be done?" said Flavia.

The doctor looked at the sick man, and Flavia followed his eyes. Nothing could be done but stand by Cassius, feeling there might be comfort in their presence, knowing there was none; nothing but watch the shortening breath, and feel their own stop, as a sudden deep sigh preceded a silence.

There was a faint stir as it came. The doctor bent over the couch. The wife and father remained with their eyes on it until they found they were alone. Voices were heard outside and seemed to liberate their own.

"I could not know, my dear. How could anyone know? This takes more of my life than yours."

"What kind of a life did Cassius have?" said Flavia, with a cry in her tones. "Did he find it worth while? Did it hold as much as other men's? Did he feel that it did? Did he ever tell you how he saw it?"

"It is no good to wish it different. It would be to wish him different, and this is not the time."

"I cannot help wishing it. It would have been better for him. I wish he had been happier. I wish he had had more. I wish I had given it to him. I had the opportunity day by day. I had it only a few hours ago, and to the end of my life I shall wish it."

"I hardly do so. I gave him what I had to give. And I do not need to talk of the end of my life. It is at its end. My son and I will be together, even if in emptiness."

"It is hard to think Cassius does not exist, harder than to think it of other men. It seems that he would be angry about it, that it ought not to have happened to him."

"Do we feel it should happen to any of us? Do our reason

164

and our feeling work together? How should they do so? We do not welcome the truth."

"We cannot know what it is."

"We cannot prove that we know it. We may cling to that."

"How good a wife do you think I was to him?"

"As good as any woman could have been. No one was the wife for Cassius. It was easier to be his father."

"What a difficult life! And yet why need it have been? He seemed to have the nature of a child and the feelings of a man. I see him like that suddenly, and feel I should always have done so."

"There is some truth in it, my dear. I said that my part was the easier."

"So I shall live without Cassius."

"And I shall die without him. And I did not look to do that. I have thought of his living without me. He is more fortunate than I, or I like to think so."

Ainger returned to the room and went up to Mr. Clare.

"May I advise you to accompany us, ma'am?" he said, as he led him to the door. "It would have been the master's wish. That is what remains to us."

They followed Ainger to the drawing-room, and saw that he was serving them with a sense of fulfilling his master's directions. It occurred to them both to wonder what these would have been.

"So you and I will be here together," said Flavia to her father-in-law. "And when you die, I shall be here alone. I shall be alone with the children. I shall deal with them alone. Cassius would have said I should have Catherine, but I shall not have her. It will be a stretch of emptiness. I do not feel I can face it."

"We are able for what we must. If our strength fails, it brings our solution. And yours will take you on. I do not say you are fortunate. You will find a barren path and you will follow it."

"Would Cassius be glad to be missed so much?"

Mr. Clare was silent, a faint smile on his lips.

"I have no wish to see Catherine," said Flavia. "I feel it was a mistake that I ever saw her."

"It was never your wish. It was thrust on you. You did your best with it, and it grew beyond you. It had to do that or fail, though at the time we did not see it. Cassius asked too much, and he got nothing. You had to give too much, and the reaction came. It was a living and growing thing."

"I shall blame myself all my life. I feel it is the one thing I shall do."

"Less with every month, and soon with every day and hour."

"I do not mean only for Catherine. I know that demand was made on me there. It was all I could do to meet it. I mean for my life with Cassius, for most of those nine years. I knew he wanted flattery. I could have given it to him. Why cannot we serve each other? Why could I not meet his need? I knew he wanted too much sympathy, and I gave too little. I had my own standard and observed it as if it were absolute. And it was only mine. Cassius was alone."

"No, I was with him. I feel I can say it. It is my drop of comfort, and I need not do without it. He was less alone than you were. You can feel that you bore the most. And if he came back to life, he would be the same. You would find the same trouble, meet the same failure. That means that you did not fail. And you did not leave him, as the other woman did. And he did not deal with you as he did with her. That is your success."

"I wish I had had a real one. But I can only have what is mine. And I hardly understand myself. My sympathy with Catherine is gone. I see her as another woman."

"I never saw her as she saw herself. It was perhaps your mistake that you did so. We should see people through our own eyes, if we keep them clear. I saw my son through mine, and loved him for himself and showed it. I have that to carry with me."

"You are the fortunate one of us, or rather you are the best."

"I have been the best to Cassius. I will take what is mine. But I knew him as a child, and saw the child in him. That was my help."

They fell into silence, and Ainger, who had stood with bent head while they spoke, noiselessly left the room.

He went to the kitchen without much thought of himself and sat down in his place. The others looked at him in some awe before his experience.

"Well, it is over, Mrs. Frost, and I feel my life is over with it. When the old gentleman is gone, I shall have nothing. It may be a mistake to be knit so close, but it comes about in spite of us. An obscure life holds its troubles."

"Is the mistress prostrate?" said Kate, as though this might be assumed.

"Her head is upright, Kate, and the old gentleman is the same. Other things about them are not to be passed on."

"Shan't we ever see the master again?" said Simon.

"No, my boy," said Ainger, with a note of full acceptance of what he said. "If you failed towards him, it is too late to rectify it now."

"And I am not an advocate for feminine rule," said Kate.

"It is the man's part," said Ainger. "He is the natural head. And I make no implication."

"No, you managed without one," said Mrs. Frost.

"I meant nothing adverse," said Ainger.

"I do not exalt the female sex," said Kate.

"We may do so, Kate, within its sphere."

"That first business was on a woman's level," said Halliday.

"Halliday, the master is dead," said Ainger, perhaps taking Kate's view.

"And the others' foolishness of not sending for the doctor!" said Halliday to Kate. "Taking matters into their own hands!"

167

"You can say it to my face, Halliday," said Ainger. "Not turn aside and say it to a woman. It is a thing I shall carry with me."

"It will accompany you to the grave," said Kate, in sad agreement.

"I shall suffer for it, though I am innocent. It is the hardest kind of trouble."

"Has the mistress uttered any word of reproach?"

"If she had, I would have heard it in silence. But she moves in her sphere. Such things would not emerge."

"You can say it to my face," said Halliday.

Madge moved her hand across her eyes.

"Ah, Madge, that is how I feel," said Ainger. "But I have to regard my sex."

"Let yourself go, Mr. Ainger," said Kate, in sympathy.

Ainger shook his head with a smile.

"There may be courage under an aspect," said Kate.

"It can be said of Mr. Clare," said Ainger. "There is an instance of a broken heart, if you want one."

"I am not sure that I do," said Mrs. Frost.

"And he will not be with us much longer," said Kate.

"He and I have followed the fortunes of the house," said Ainger. "We have stood, as it were, outside. The master and I stand together within it."

"You should use the past tense," said Kate.

"So I should; so I must by degrees. It comes hard to my tongue to use the word, 'was', of the master."

"We know he would not return, if he could."

"We may know it, Kate, with our heads. In my heart I shall always feel that he would revisit the old haunts, if he could."

"Was he good enough to go where it is better than here?" said Simon.

"It is not for you to enquire after those above you," said Ainger.

"And now so much above," said Mrs. Frost.

"Mrs. Frost, I should not have instanced it as a case for pleasantry. I wonder at its striking you in that light."

"We cannot have only heaviness," said Kate.

"There is nothing else for me," said Ainger. "For me it is one of the passages. I go alone through it, and would not include others. I have had the gain and accept the loss. We pay the price."

"Of every happiness," said Kate. "Perhaps still waters are best."

"The master was not very old," said Madge.

"Fifty-two summers," said Ainger. "It was his weakness to pass for less, or we will say his whim. But for me the veil was lifted."

"To me he looked his age," said Kate.

"His face carried the ravages of his experience. And I do not share his reluctance. Forty is my age, and as forty I stand before you. It is the right age for a man. But this will take me forward. Middle age is in sight."

"I am sixty-three and not troubled by it," said Halliday.

"Seven years from the span," said Kate.

"And not troubled by that!" said Mrs. Frost.

"Our time has to come," said Halliday.

"That is what I mean," said Mrs. Frost. "And it is what the master meant."

"Mrs. Frost, had you no feeling for the master?" said Ainger.

"I had as much as he had for me."

"He estimated your skill in your line, and indeed gave voice to it. He was not conversant with your life in its other aspects."

"He did not know it had any."

"Now, Mrs. Frost, how could he?"

"He could not, as it had none."

"Now, Mrs. Frost, you cannot expect us to believe that."

"I daresay the master would have believed it, if he had thought about me."

"Now how often did you think about him, apart from matters in your sphere? And of those he spoke in commendation. And I lost no time in conveying it to you."

"We have to be thankful for small mercies," said Madge.

"I am not," said Mrs. Frost. "They are too small."

"Mrs. Frost preserves her note," said Kate.

"I did not suspect her of principles of equality," said Ainger.

"There is the order of things," said Kate.

"I used to wish to advance," said Ainger. "And it may raise its head. For the moment I find it enough to have served."

"I am glad your sorrow is to be short-lived," said Mrs. Frost.

"Mrs. Frost, you fail to do Mr. Ainger justice," said Kate.

"Ah, never mind, Kate," said Ainger. "I do not stake any claims. No, Simon, you may keep your seat. The bell is my prerogative to-day. I feel it is my heritage from the master. It comes to me as a bequest."

"It is his legacy to you," said Kate.

"I would rather have the ordinary kind," said Mrs. Frost.

"Well, Mrs. Frost, if you want to know, you have it," said Ainger, pausing and speaking almost fiercely. "The master has remembered both you and me in his will. He reposed his trust in me on the point. And the others benefit to a proportionate extent, priority receiving its due."

"But Mrs. Frost spoke without ulterior thought," said Kate.

"So now you know what to think of him," said Ainger.

"So I do," said Mrs. Frost, "and I am thinking it. But I did not know before."

"I am glad I did not speak against him," said Kate. "Not that it should exert an influence."

"I never will again," said Mrs. Frost. "I find it is exerting one."

"I have been here nearly fifty years, boy and man," said Halliday. "If things are to be taken into account."

"So that is your instinctive response," said Ainger. "Surely the amount is negligible."

"I hope not," said Mrs. Frost.

"Mrs. Frost, I meant it was secondary, as you know."

"It is the thought," said Kate.

"But the thought must have an object," said Halliday.

"I am in a position to state figures," said Ainger. "But I refrain from doing so. It is not the occasion. I was wrong to broach the topic."

"You did it to uphold the master," said Kate.

"It must emerge in the end," said Halliday. "It is not your secret."

"That will seem strange to me, when it has been so for so long."

"You must sometimes have felt the impulse to divulge it," said Kate.

"You are mistaken, Kate. It was dependent on the master's passing. I held my thoughts apart."

"If he had lived the normal time, I should have gone before him," said Halliday. "There would have been no reward for a lifetime."

"Anyone would think it was the matter of the moment," said Ainger. "I regret that it escaped me."

"I suppose it was meant to interest us."

"It was meant for that, Halliday. The master thought of our advantage at the time when he would have nothing. There is something that grips the heart."

"People have to make their wills. They are not heroes for that."

"I think they are," said Mrs. Frost. "I made my will, and I was a hero."

"You can't take anything with you."

"I said I was a hero."

"The master had choice," said Ainger. "He could have left everything to the family without further thought."

"Perhaps they are heroes," said Mrs. Frost. "I hope they are."

"Oh, it is not on that scale," said Halliday.

"There is the bell again, Mr. Ainger," said Kate, in surprise at Ainger's delay.

"It is strange," said the latter, standing straight and still, "how I miss something in the master's ring, something firm and masculine that spoke from him to me——" He turned and vanished as the bell rang again.

"Something firm and feminine spoke to him," said Mrs. Frost.

"That is what we have now," said Halliday. "And we shall have more of it."

"Aren't ladies as good as men?" said Simon.

"They tend to be subject to themselves," said Kate.

"And that means other people are subject to them," said Halliday.

"If ever anyone carried a grief, it is Mr. Ainger," said Kate. "The way he does not protrude it tells its tale. His presence should act as a restraint."

"Ah, we are a thought worked up," said Halliday.

"The note of hysteria," said Kate. "We must not judge each other."

"Mr. Ainger judged me," said Mrs. Frost.

"I can imagine his bearing as he reaches the drawing-room," said Kate. "It would stand as an example."

Ainger was doing his best to make it do so.

"Yes, ma'am? Yes, sir?" he said, without raising his eyes.

"There are messages to be taken," said Mr. Clare.

"I have seen that the word is passed, sir."

"And directions to be given. Your mistress must be spared."

"I was not proposing to approach her, sir. Matters are on foot."

"And the children should be told," said Flavia. "They must not hear from anyone but me."

"Then it should be soon, ma'am. Ill news travels apace."

"Perhaps you will bring them to us."

"If I may suggest it, ma'am, would not their own quarters be the right background?"

"What do you think?" said Flavia, to her father-in-law.

"I should say that those are better without the memory. We cannot make it a good one."

"It is a point of view, sir," said Ainger, turning to the door.

"Only our own," said Mr. Clare, "but we will hold to it. As the young man dealt with my son, so will I deal with him. But he must fill his own place."

CHAPTER XIII

T HE CHILDREN ENTERED the room, their faces pale with apprehension. The change in the atmosphere of the house had seemed to come to meet them. Henry and Megan hung back, as though in fear of some ordeal. Bennet closed the door and remained within it, not withdrawing the support of her presence.

"My little ones," said Flavia, opening her arms to the five, "I have something sad to tell you, something so sad that you will not guess what it is."

"Is it Father?" said Megan at once. "Didn't he get better this time?"

"My little girl, it is Father. But this time was not like the last. He had an ordinary illness and did not recover."

"Is he dead?" said Guy. "Shan't we ever see him again?"

"You will not, my little son. You only have your mother now."

"Fabian and Guy have another mother," said Henry, after a pause. "That will make it better for them. They still have two parents. They are not left with only one."

"Yes, it gives them more to depend on. But it will not make up for their father. This is a trouble we must all share together."

Toby looked enquiringly from face to face, and Flavia took him on her knee and rested her cheek against his.

"My baby boy, you always loved your father."

"Yes, Toby love him. Not Henry and Guy."

"Yes, you all loved him."

"No, only Toby."

"Father has gone to sleep and will not wake up any more."

"Oh, yes," said Toby, getting off her knee. "Toby lie down too. But both quite well again."

"Where has Father gone?" said Henry.

"No one can know that."

"I don't think he wanted to go away from here," said Megan. "I think he liked it better than he thought."

"Did his illness hurt him?" said Henry, causing his sister to shrink into herself.

"No, not at all," said his mother. "He just felt ill and tired."

"Was he a very old man?"

"No, only middle-aged. He will never know what it is to be old."

Fabian came up and laid his hand on his stepmother's shoulder, and Guy began to weep and threw himself against her.

"I haven't had a mother like other boys. And now I haven't a father. Why does it have to be like that?"

Flavia kept him within her arm, and Toby soberly regarded the occupation of his place.

"Eliza says people go to heaven when they die," said Henry. "But only if they are good enough."

"Father was good enough," said Megan. "Everyone is supposed to be in heaven, and they can't all be better than he was. And I think he was better than he seemed to be."

"Anyhow he wasn't bad enough to go anywhere else."

"Hush, hush," said Bennet. "He loved you very much, and that is all you need to know."

"I suppose there are different kinds of love. Some of them almost seem like something else."

"We can only love according to ourselves," said Fabian, speaking for the first time. "We cannot alter our natures."

"We still have Bennet," said Megan, in a voice that just disclaimed despair.

"She might die at any time," said Henry. "She is nearly as old as Father."

"No, I shall not die. You need not think about that."

"This makes you think about things. Grandpa would have been a better person to die."

"It is the truth, my boy," said Mr. Clare.

"Do you wish you had died instead of Father?"

"It would have been my choice, if I had had one."

Megan ceased to struggle with her tears, and Guy moved towards her and they wept together.

"Toby not cry," said the latter. "Very brave boy."

"A child, ma'am!" said Ainger. "He thinks as a child and understands as a child. It is not his time to put away childish things."

"I feel I have hardly done so until to-day," said Flavia.

"I have something of the same feeling, ma'am."

"Did Father know he made so much difference?" said Henry. "If he had known, he might have tried to make more."

"It is we who know it, sir," said Ainger.

"Is it possible that he knows?" said Guy.

"I should say it is probable, sir, if not a certainty."

"Shall we still have to come down after luncheon?" said Henry to his mother.

"Yes, things will be just as Father had them. We shall make no difference."

"That is done for us, ma'am," said Ainger.

"We shan't be poorer, shall we? Like some people when the father is dead? Father didn't earn any money."

"He was not called upon to do so, sir," said Ainger.

"Do you mind his being dead?"

"As much as I could mind anything, sir."

"But he was not your relation."

"He was always a friend to me, sir."

"We are glad that Ainger feels with us," said Flavia.

"Neither of you seems very different," said Henry.

"Still waters run deep, sir," said Ainger. "Not that I make claims or aspire to comparisons."

"Do people feel more, the less they show it?" said Megan.

"We have to suppress ourselves, miss. It is the braver course."

"Bravery seems to be more for other people than for yourself," said Henry.

"That is what constitutes it, sir."

"Did Father wish we had loved him more than we did?" said Guy.

"He knew he was not easy to understand," said Flavia. "He would hardly have expected children to understand him."

"He seemed to expect it," said Henry. "And I think we did understand him, or anyhow Megan did. That may make it better for her now. Shall we have the same life upstairs?"

"Yes, that will not be different. But you will not feel it is the same."

"Why shan't we, if it is?"

"Ah, sir, time will show you," said Ainger. "You need not go to meet it."

"I suppose you are a widow," said Henry to his mother. "Is Fabian's mother a widow too, or can there only be one?"

"There can only be one," said Megan. "There could only be one wife."

"What is Grandpa?" said Henry.

"There is no word for it, my boy," said Mr. Clare.

"What am I, sir?" said Ainger. "There is no word for it either."

"Would Father be surprised by people's minding his dying so much?"

"I think he might be," said Megan. "I think people liked him better than he knew."

"Ah, miss, we find that, when a call comes," said Ainger.

"I wish he had known how much I liked him," said Megan.

"I don't think I wish it," said Henry. "I am not sure how much I did. Sometimes I liked him better than at other times. And he seemed the same with me."

"When I am older, I shan't have a father," said Megan. "And when I am a woman, I shan't have one. And some people have one always."

"A sad case, ma'am. But this is even sadder," said Ainger, as Toby went past. "He will not remember the master."

"I almost wish I didn't remember him," said Henry. "Then I could think things were better than they were. Perhaps I shall forget."

"I think he loved us more than he seemed to," said Guy. "It seems that a person's dying makes you know more about him."

"Out of the mouth of babes, ma'am!" said Ainger.

"I think it makes you exaggerate things," said Henry. "The good part of him and the bad part of yourself."

"Again there is truth in it, ma'am."

"We wish we had been different," said Fabian. "But if the person came back, we should be the same."

Ainger smiled at his mistress in lieu of words.

"And the person would be the same too," said Henry.

"Poor boy!" said Mr. Clare to himself.

"Was Father really a boy to Grandpa?" said Henry.

"We are always children to our parents," said Flavia.

"He was a child to me," said Mr. Clare. "He saw me as he always had. For me it is a man's and a woman's grief."

"Would Father have minded losing you as much as you mind losing him?" said Henry.

"No, it would have been in the order of things. But I am wrong. He would have minded as much."

"That is the line of my own thought, sir," said Ainger.

"I think the children should come upstairs now," said Bennet.

Toby turned and ran towards the door.

"Good-bye, Ainger; good-bye, Father," he said, waving his hand.

"Father is not there any more," said Bennet.

"Not there any more. So Toby say good-bye."

They all went together to the nursery, the elder boys yielding to the instinct to relapse into childhood. They found Miss Ridley awaiting them, and accepted her presence as her tribute to the occasion.

"Well, shall I read to you all?" she said, in a tone of subdued cheerfulness.

"I would rather talk," said Fabian.

"What is there to talk about?" said Henry. "There is the one thing, and we have talked about that."

"Can Father see us now?" said Megan.

"Yes, all the time," said Bennet.

"Can he hear us?" said Henry. "And see into our hearts?"

"It is better to do what he would wish," said Miss Ridley, "and to leave that kind of question."

"Why do we talk as if he was so much better than he was? Was he such a very good man?"

"I think perhaps he was in his heart," said Guy.

"You may be quite right, Guy," said Miss Ridley. "That is what I think."

"Goodness in the heart isn't much use to people," said Henry. "It would be better almost anywhere else."

There was some amusement that was immediately checked.

"Is it wrong to laugh to-day?" said Henry, on a ruthless note.

"It is not very suitable," said Miss Ridley. "And we do not feel inclined to do so."

"Are we supposed never to be happy again?"

"No, of course you are not," said Bennet. "Father would want you to be happy."

"He didn't seem to want it. Sometimes he threw a gloom

over us. Oughtn't we to speak the truth about someone who is dead?"

"We should speak the whole truth," said Fabian. "Not only the worse part of it."

"We are supposed to speak only good," said Guy.

"Then there would be some people we could not speak about at all."

"If I could choose one thing," said Megan, in a tone that showed she had not heard, "it would be to have Father alive again."

"I am sure it would," said Bennet.

"Why are you sure?" said Henry. "He didn't make much difference to her. Sometimes he made her cry."

"But only because he felt in that mood," said Megan. "Not because in his heart he wanted to."

"We had a father like that," said Henry, "and now we haven't one at all. Oh, dear, oh, dear!"

"Now I thought we had come to the end of that," said Eliza.

"Some things can't come to an end. Things happen that make them begin again."

"I think it is natural to say it to-day," said Bennet, accepting any sign of conventional feeling.

"How nicely Toby is playing by himself!" said Eliza, who had not lost hold of life in its ordinary aspects.

"Shall we see Mater again before we go to bed?" said Henry. "There doesn't seem any reason."

"She will come up to say good-night to you," said Miss Ridley.

"She doesn't always."

"I am sure she will to-night."

"Tell her Toby play by himself," said Toby, pulling at Eliza's sleeve.

As Flavia crossed the hall on her way to the staircase, a figure moved from behind it.

"I heard an hour ago. I have a word to say. I have come at once to say it. You must foresee it. You shall not have it before you. I came into your life and broke it. I can only withdraw. Cassius gave me what he could. I took all he had. I was too sunk in myself to know it. I am guilty in all eyes. I am guilty indeed in yours. I am most guilty in my own. I felt it when Cassius was ill the first time. Now I feel it enough to say it. I am leaving the place. I will not stay to harass you. I will not add to the remorse that is yours and mine. It will be mine to the end. But that is no help to you. I can help you by leaving you. I will give you that help."

"How about the boys?" said Flavia, as though this were all that need be said, and protest or question were out of place.

"I have no right to answer that question. I have forfeited the right. I took everything for myself. I will take what I am given."

"If you leave the place, they must choose between you and me. They must either go with you or make this house their home. There can be no middle course. It is for them to decide."

"I see that it is. I do not deserve that it should be. I do not deserve their free judgement and choice. I should have had a right to ask it, if I had asked no more. I will not think what I asked and took."

"I am going to them now. I will find out what they choose; this life or another, your home or mine. It is better for me to ask them. I am still the familiar figure and shall meet the natural response."

"I will not stand between you. I will not even stand aside. I will wait or return, as you bid me."

"You may wait," said Flavia, in an empty tone. "It is what I should do in your place."

She went upstairs, a listless figure, while Catherine stood, vital and tense, below. The force that emanated from her seemed to be held in bonds to herself.

Flavia approached the children as though she hardly saw them, as though held by her thought. Bennet stood with grave eyes, stricken by the thought of further strain on them. Miss Ridley put a chair for Flavia in tribute to her bereavement. The latter sat down and beckoned to the elder boys.

"My sons, I have to ask you one thing, and to ask you to tell me the truth. It is a turning-point in your lives. Your mother is leaving the place; I mean your own mother. Do you choose to go with her or to stay here with me? Take your time and think only of the truth."

"Stay here with you," said Guy at once, "where we have always been."

"Take your time, Fabian, and keep your mind on the truth. You are not responsible for it."

"It is a hard question," said her stepson, after a pause that told of obedience rather than need. "We must be drawn in two ways. You have been the mother of our childhood, and that seems to be the greatest thing. But our childhood will pass. And only a real mother can be a mother to me. The time will get nearer and nearer. We must think of the whole of our lives."

"You choose to go with your own mother?"

"Yes, I choose that."

Guy spoke through tears and threw his arms round his stepmother.

"I don't want to leave you. I don't want to go away from you. I don't want anyone as much as I want you. I shall never be glad I have left you. Not even when I have a real mother, not even when I am a man. But I must go with Fabian. To live without him would be the same as being dead."

Flavia answered in an even tone, almost as though she were quoting the words.

"You are right to make the honest choice. And it may be the wise one. We shall always have our feeling for each other. It will always remain between us. I shall be the mother of your childhood, as you will be the sons of my youth. If there is nothing else, it is enough."

Guy's voice came in a shaken whisper, audible only to Flavia and himself.

"But I shall be a boy for a long time. And a mother does not matter so much to men."

"Are Fabian and Guy going to leave us?" said Megan, whose eyes had been fixed on the scene. "To leave us as well as Father?"

"My poor little girl, it is a time of change indeed."

"Aren't they ever coming back?" said Henry. "There is not much meaning in a family, if it breaks apart."

"Not to live with us. They will come to see us, of course."

"And each time they come they will be different," said Megan. "And each time we shall be different too. And at last we shall be too different to know each other."

In the pause that followed, Bennet's was the silence that spoke.

Flavia returned to Catherine and found her quiet and still, as though she had no right to impatience. She lifted her eyes at once, keeping them under her command.

"They choose to go with you," said Flavia. "Or rather Fabian chooses it, and Guy will go with his brother."

"He chooses you as his mother?"

"Yes, he chooses me as that."

"I am glad he does. I do not take everything. I leave as much as I take. I am glad it is yours. I am glad he gives it to you. You and I are equal to each other."

"I hope he will not suffer," said Flavia, as if her thought broke out. "He is so young. What if things go hard with him?"

"I will talk to him of you. He shall talk of you to me. I will see you through his eyes. I will always do so. He shall come to you without me between you. I will see I am never that. And with Fabian it shall be the same. I know by what a feeble thread I hold him."

"He feels he will need his own mother when he is a man. He is old enough to see the future."

"Do you not see it too?" said Catherine, in her quick,

low tones. "Do you not see the further time? When you will have your children by themselves, without those of another woman? As it is natural for you to have them. As it is natural for you to be seen with them. Is there not, will there not be, a recompense there?"

Flavia looked into her face, and there seemed to be a third presence in the hall, the difference between them.

CHAPTER XIV

"Where is Catherine?" said Elton to his sister. "Has she gone to sympathise with Flavia?"

"No, she feels she has no right to do so. I think she has gone to take leave of her."

"Has anything happened to their friendship?"

"I believe it has come to an end with Cassius. It seems to have somehow depended on him."

"Then will she always be at home with us?"

"You can think for yourself. Don't you see her eyes rest on us in compunction and pity?"

"Ursula, do you realise what your words imply?"

"Well, I hardly dare to do so."

"Has she any real feeling for us?"

"She has the right feeling and conquers any other. She is true to her vision of herself. She is really true to it."

"What was the bond between her and Flavia, apart from their experience with Cassius?"

"They wanted no other. That gave them the scope they needed. They could pity and suffer and forgive."

"So you are on Cassius's side?"

"Well, he is dead, and when he was alive, he could not live with my sister."

"Considering what we owe to the dead, and that everyone dies," said Elton, "it is a wonder we manage as well as we do. And we do a good deal for the living, considering we owe them nothing. But have we done anything for Catherine?"

"We have simply gone on living with each other. I have been afraid she would notice it."

"Does she think she is necessary to us?"

"It has not occurred to her that she could not be."

"Have you ever seen an expression cross my face, that reminded you of her?"

"Well, I have not spoken of it, as I have seen the same thing in the glass. But you may speak of it. It will be easier to bear it together."

"Does it mean a likeness underneath?"

"No, it is only skin-deep, as beauty would be, if we had it. It is fair that they should be the same."

"Do you think we have qualities in common? Are we all prone to admire ourselves?"

"No, you and I live over a deep uncertainty. And Catherine does not admire herself until she has arranged some reason for doing so."

"She is coming up the path," said Elton. "And I don't think she has arranged any reason. Can it be that for an hour she has been without one?"

"I should hardly think for as much as an hour," said Ursula.

Catherine came into the room and paused in her usual way.

"I have done it. I have been to my friend. I have broken our friendship. It was a strange one. Good has not come of it. It is time for it to end."

"I thought that friendships died of themselves," said Elton, "and that no one could explain it."

"Perhaps this one has done so. Perhaps it carried its death knell in it. It may be that ordinary things are the right stuff of life."

"Well, that would explain life as we find it," said Ursula.

"We tried to steer a course beyond them. We thought we could do what others could not do."

"Don't we always think that?"

"We should not act upon it."

"I did not know we ever did."

"I did, and harm came of it. I harmed the man who was once my husband. I harmed him when he tried to

186

serve me. And I thought I could not harm anyone. The common words are true. Pride goes before a fall."

"It goes after it," said her sister. "A fall involves tragedy, and it is so dignified to suffer."

"But not to cause suffering."

"Perhaps that is tragedy at its height."

"Humiliation at its depth," said Catherine, standing with her hands clasped. "The image of Cassius lives with me. Cassius harmed by his own hand, and that hand really mine. Cassius lying dead as the result of my return to his life."

"Surely that is not true," said Ursula.

"The one thing followed from the other. I caused the first trouble, and but for that, help would have come in the second. I will not turn from the truth."

"I will," said Elton. "I see we were wrong about Cassius. But I will not be brave enough to admit it. Moral courage drags one down."

"He was not like other men," said Ursula. "We are supposed to think that of ourselves, and we think it of him. But Catherine was not to blame for his nature."

"Was he to blame for it?" said her sister. "It had its claim. I knew him. We had cause to know each other. Knowing me, he served me to the end of his power. How did I serve him?"

"Service is too much for anyone. It seems that people either fail in it or that it ends in their death. And we have to take the blame for our natures. Elton and I have always done so."

"Their demand should be met. It is the basis of human intercourse."

"That is at the bottom of everything. It is odd that we do not try to manage without it."

"It constitutes human life. And I have failed in it."

"Well, we all fail in life," said Ursula.

"We miss success. But that does not matter."

"Do you really think Elton and I have missed it?"

"And that it does not matter?" said her brother.

"You are good to me. You would lift my burden. But it is mine. I must carry it."

"Would it hurt anyone if you cast it down?"

"It would hurt myself. It would harden my heart. And its hardness had done enough. I must suffer what I must."

"You make too much of it," said Elton. "Cassius had had a great deal of his life."

"Not as much as you think at your age."

"I am one of those people who have never been young."

"And I am sure I am one of those who were never a child," said Ursula.

"I remember you both as children."

"We are talking of our memory of ourselves."

"Don't you think you are making changes in it?"

"Well, only for the better," said Ursula.

"You were never old for your ages."

"Well, we should hardly have been precocious."

"I almost think you were behind them."

"Well, we may have been the kind of people to develop late."

"Cassius was not of the age to die," said Catherine.

"What is the age?" said her sister.

"About seventy," said Elton, "when we have had our span, and people have not begun to think less of us."

"Do you think less of old people?" said Catherine.

"No, I admire them for having had their lives and being sure of them. But that is rare. Most people despise them for not being able to eat their cake and have it, even though it is only the chance of it."

"Do you feel that life is so uncertain?"

"Well, I feel that mine is safe. But I like to talk of the uncertainty; it sounds so brave."

"It is braver than not being able to speak of it at all, like most people," said Ursula. "Speaking of a thing makes it real, and that does mean too much with such a subject."

"So much in life needs courage," said Catherine.

"Almost everything," said her sister. "We even talk of daring to be ourselves. Though I expect we mean daring to show ourselves, and naturally that would need it."

"Some people dare to do that," said Elton, "though you might not believe it. Think of Miss Ridley."

"Must we think of her?" said Ursula. "She shows a cheerful spirit, and she may be homeless at any moment."

"If I were a governess," said Elton, "and I do not mean a tutor, people would not feel the house was home without me. So the power would be mine, and I should use it."

"Well, if you did not, what good would it be? People think it natural to want power, and wrong to exercise it. They are inconsistent, or rather they have grudging hearts. I expect it is the same thing."

"It is hard to say where power has lain in that house," said Catherine.

"What a dark way you speak of it!" said Elton.

"You forget it was once my home."

"Well, there is nothing to remind me of it."

"I was always an alien. I felt less so when I returned. And now I am an alien again. There is nothing to hold me to it. My link with it was Cassius, although we were estranged. Not Flavia, although we were friends. I ought to have eschewed that friendship. I see it was a furtive thing."

"We could not eschew things because of that," said Ursula. "We should have to give up so many of our small pleasures; some of them because they were so small."

"Tell me one of them," said Elton.

"Feeling superior to Miss Ridley, because my position is better than hers."

"Why is it better?" said Catherine. "It is not more respected."

"Things that we do not respect, like money and ease and leisure, are such good things. And we should respect them, if we were allowed to."

189

"Miss Ridley will stay on with the younger children. They have to be prepared for life."

"Life has to be what it is," said Elton, "but fancy preparing people for it! It seems like helping it all to go on."

"Why do we feel that governesses are not like other people?" said Ursula.

"They begin like other people, and are moulded by their life, as we all are," said her sister. "I have a particular respect for them."

"Oh, I don't really respect anyone else. Perhaps that is what I meant."

"You should not mean things," said Elton. "You ought to be above it."

"Did Cassius respect Miss Ridley?" said Ursula.

"I believe he would have found her a friend, if he had thought of it," said Catherine.

"I did not know he was so unmanly," said Elton.

"How much will the children miss him?" said Ursula.

"I do not know their life behind the scenes."

"I should think they will miss him more than that," said Elton. "How much will Flavia do so?"

"I cannot tell you," said Catherine.

"You have told me," said her brother.

"You claim to read too much into people's words. The line seems to strike you as a good one."

"Catherine, do not throw off all disguise. I cannot bear people to stand exposed."

"Does Flavia suffer from remorse?" said Ursula.

"If we speak of remorse, I can only think of my own."

"But try to think of Flavia's. I want a complete picture."

"Are you interested or only curious?" said Catherine.

"I do not know the difference, and I do not believe there is any."

"Is your heart involved or only your head?"

"Well, I like to be purely intellectual."

"Then I will not tell you. And Elton need not say I have done so."

"No, there is no need," said her brother.

"Why are we talking in this way?"

"It is to stave something off," said Elton. "I do not dare say what."

"I must dare to," said Catherine, again clasping her hands. "It is the word about the future. I have had to face the truth. My presence here is harmful. I will do no more harm. I have to break something to you. Something that does harm to you. I seem to live to cause it."

"You are going to leave us," said Elton.

"You are good to me. You save me the words. I wish I could be good to you. From my heart I wish it. But I must go from this place. I am a menace to it. I have to say it of myself. For years I deserted you. I have to desert you again."

"Do you feel you can leave the boys?" said Ursula.

"I felt I could not. But it was no matter what I felt. It was a thing of no account. I asked Flavia to advise me. To direct me; I would have obeyed. She asked my sons to choose between her and me."

"And they chose their own mother?" said Ursula.

"Fabian did so. Guy chose to go with his brother. In his heart he chose his stepmother. It is for me to see that in his heart he always chooses her."

"Would it not be better for him to transfer the feeling to you?"

"I have no claim. I ask for nothing. I am to have too much. I fear the kindness of fate. I have feared it before. It seems I am to live in the fear."

"It should be a good life," said Elton. "How soon will you be embarking on it? We must accept the truth."

"My brother, it must be soon. To wait would again do harm. My sons must make the change at once. To look forward to it is to suffer. And Flavia and I must part. We have parted in spirit. And I would not stay, if I could. I have become a sinister presence. And now I will thank you and leave you. You have things to talk of together."

"We have one thing," said Elton, as the door closed, "our life without Catherine. They say that things are never the same a second time, but this will be the same. I shall pour out the tea, and you will order the house."

"But we shall not see a human story unfolding before our eyes."

"And ending in tragedy. I know we shall miss all that."

"Are you afraid of Catherine? Do you believe what she says of herself?"

"I believe part of it. So of course I am afraid. And she does not believe even part of what we say of ourselves, and that makes me more so."

"Do you believe it all yourself?"

"Well, we are known to be sometimes surprised by ourselves."

"I don't think we often are. Even less often than by other people. So we are glad that Catherine is going."

"Ought we to be as much surprised by ourselves as that?"

"She sees the life she wanted, opening before her. It seems a good deal for someone who asks nothing."

"But we do not feel she ought not to take it," said Elton. "We should have to be too much surprised."

"Whom are you sorriest for in the whole sad tale?"

"Cassius, because he is dead. Guy has lost a mother; Flavia a friend; the children have lost a father. But he has lost himself."

"It would not be so bad to be nothing," said Ursula.

"You know that to be something would be better."

"Would it, with the temperament of Cassius?"

"I will not be a person who says we cannot wish it otherwise, when someone has died."

"Then you will be unique."

"Yes, I shall," said Elton.